BY MARISSA MULLEN

That Cheese Plate Wants to Party

That Cheese Plate Will Change Your Life

That Cheese Plate
Wants to Party

That Cheese Plate
—
Wants to Party

Festive Boards, Spreads,
and Recipes with the
Cheese By Numbers Method

Marissa Mullen

Illustrated by Sara Gilanchi

THE DIAL PRESS • NEW YORK

Published in the United States by The Dial Press,
an imprint of Random House, a division
of Penguin Random House LLC, New York.

THE DIAL PRESS is a registered trademark
and the colophon is a trademark of
Penguin Random House LLC.

LIBRARY OF CONGRESS CATALOGING-IN-PUBLICATION DATA
Names: Mullen, Marissa, author. | Gilanchi, Sara, illustrator.
Title: That cheese plate wants to party: festive boards, spreads,
and recipes with the cheese by numbers method /
Marissa Mullen; illustrated by Sara Gilanchi.
Description: New York: The Dial Press, [2023] |
Includes index.
Identifiers: LCCN 2022039276 (print) | LCCN 2022039277
(ebook) | ISBN 9780593446683 (hardcover) |
ISBN 9780593446690 (ebook)
Subjects: LCSH: Cheese—Varieties. | Appetizers. |
Cooking (Cheese). | Cocktails. | LCGFT: Cookbooks.
Classification: LCC TX382 .M8495 2023 (print) |
LCC TX382 (ebook) | DDC 641.6/73—dc23/eng/20220817
LC record available at https://lccn.loc.gov/2022039276
LC ebook record available at https://lccn.loc.gov/2022039277

Photograph on page i: Lauren Andrade
Photographs on pages 13, 30, 66, 262, and 272: Noel McGrath
Photographs on pages 6, 16, 17, 18, and 102–103: Lucas Stevenson
Photograph on page 20: Michelle Baumval
Photograph on page 274: Marissa Bobkowski
Photograph on page 275: Nikki Krecicki
Printed in China on acid-free paper
randomhousebooks.com

2 4 6 8 9 7 5 3 1

FIRST EDITION
Illustrations: Sara Gilanchi
Book design by Barbara M. Bachman

*To my online community
of cheese lovers, who are always
down to party together or apart*

contents

contents

Recipes

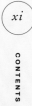

That Cheese Plate

Wants to Party

introduction

Parties. There's a reason we love them, look forward to them, and use them to mark the big occasions in our lives.

There's nothing as special to me as the positive energy of human connection and the spark of a conversation—all surrounding that cheese plate, of course. And while I'll never say no to dancing into the night or throwing an elaborate birthday bash, I've come to realize that a party should be less of an actual event and more of a mindset. If you're in the mood to celebrate life, anything can be a party.

The word *party,* to me, is very personal. It's when you can literally be "a part" of something. You can throw a party for one, relaxing after a long day with your favorite wedge of soft-ripened goat cheese and a dollop of fruit preserves. A party for two can be a date night, or lunch with a friend. A party could happen outdoors in the garden, with fresh-picked produce and local cheeses, or it could be on the stoop of your apartment building, with grocery-store finds and wine in paper cups. No matter the size, occasion, or setting, it's all about the intention behind the gathering. Parties ignite joy, connection, and conversation.

As you might have guessed, food is by far my favorite element of any party. I love how food always tells a story. Cheese, the foundation of every cheese plate, has a rich, vast history while also inspiring strong personal feelings. Some people love the bite of blue cheese, and some hate it. You might still remember a particularly delicious caprese sandwich you once had, and every time you eat fresh, creamy mozzarella you think about where you were when you ate that sandwich, whom you were with, and how good it tasted. Your feelings on any particular cheese could be as simple as "I like it," but even that shows a glimpse of who you are. Cheese plates ignite the senses, open doors for interactions, and can settle you into a self-care mood.

You might be familiar with the Cheese By Numbers method, which I created to help simplify the plating process. We break the cheese plate down into six steps: cheese, meat, produce, crunch, dip, and garnish. This method helps you slow down and take the guesswork out of what can look like an intimidating creation, so you can have fun and appreciate the art of charcuterie and cheese.

Ironically, publishing my first cookbook was the opposite of slowing down. I found myself constantly in the kitchen, planning events and creating content around the clock. Because of an unforeseen pandemic (spoiler alert), everything came to a screeching halt. Suddenly, parties were canceled, and everything that was once communal and in-person became individual and online. During this difficult time, I tried to shift my focus to what was important—the very things I had been neglecting while using busywork as a distraction. I truly connected with my community on so-cial media, hosting cheese plate happy hours on Instagram and sharing plate ideas to make at home. I then moved into my first apartment by myself, as a single gal in her late twenties, and finally learned to love my alone time. I also realized how precious time spent with friends and family could be, and cherished being together, whatever form that took. I immersed myself in nature, learning to grow my own garnishes for my plate creations and using my senses to explore the world around me. After this period of isolation and introspection, I was ready to look at the world through a new lens. I never again want to take for granted the beauty of bringing people together. The energy of togetherness should be celebrated.

This book is about turning self-care communal: celebrating the people around us and using the food we put on the table to tell our stories. We'll start with single-serve and small plate ideas, then build to the luxury grazing tables to impress the guests. We'll make themed plates, delicious recipes, and cocktails. We'll even learn how to match the colors of our tablescapes and floral arrangements to our culinary creations. Cheers to a new chapter. After all: That cheese plate wants to party!

party prep

I've been hosting "cheese parties" in my home since college. What started as a few friends around a wooden table in my tiny Boston apartment later

transformed into massive gatherings in New York City after I graduated. We had friends inviting friends, cheese plates galore, and endless conversations. No matter the size of the party, I wanted the space to have a specific feeling. I always had a curated playlist queued up, the soft glow of candles, and cheese plates set up on the table, interspersed with flowers and every serving utensil I could find. I never had the finest china, or even fancy chargers or decorations—I just used what I had in my kitchen and let ambience flow from the cheese plate.

With a few simple styling techniques, a cheese plate can set a cohesive theme for any gathering. We eat with our eyes first, so when it comes to plating, the visual effect is the initial draw. A colorful, vibrant creation with different textures and interesting focal points will make for a strong first impression. I love to use symmetry on my plates, balancing the colors and ingredients across the board. It's also important to consider the type of gathering you're throwing. The plate's composition, the design of the tablescape, and the lighting all play important roles in setting a specific mood. If I'm about to dive into a baked camembert next to a fireplace or at a candlelit dinner, it will feel and taste much more decadent than eating the same dish in a stark, fluorescent kitchen!

cheese by numbers

If the cheese plate is the center of attention at the party, make sure your creation is dressed for the occasion! Each element of the Cheese By Numbers method acts as a guest at the party, mingling together to create wonderful conversation and lively pairings.

The Cheese By Numbers method will be your best friend/guru while you craft your cheese plate. I created this method to take the stress and guesswork out of designing a beautiful plate, so you can sit back, relax, and enjoy hosting your gathering. The method consists of six steps:

1—CHEESE
2—MEAT
3—PRODUCE
4—CRUNCH
5—DIP
6—GARNISH

Taste is the most important factor of a cheese plate, and a great pairing should highlight all of the senses. With each plate I curate, I use the Cheese By Numbers method to cover the five main flavor profiles: salty, sweet, bitter, sour, and umami. I always begin with the cheese itself as the basis for each pairing.

Cheese: Cheese is (of course!) the most important part of the Cheese By Numbers method, and provides the most complex flavors to build upon. I usually feature three to five cheeses on my plates, which provide plenty of options for pairings. A variety of cheeses can consist of different milks (cow, goat, sheep, plant-based) and textures (hard, semi-hard, soft, fresh, bloomy). Check out the cheese flavor flow chart on page 22 for countless styles of cheese to consider.

Meat: I find that cured meats like salami, prosciutto, and soppressata, which are rich and savory, pair well with many cheeses, complementing the natural saltiness and fattiness. They're classics for a reason! For example, I love the combination of a delicate prosciutto with a creamy fresh mozzarella, or even an aged cheese like pecorino. You can also experiment with other flavor combinations, pairing cheese with meats like sausage, smoked salmon, and even grilled chicken!

Produce: For produce, I like to play with sweet, sour, and bitter flavor elements. Something like a briny cornichon will be able to cut through a rich cheese like a velvety raclette, while sweet, yet tangy raspberry will enhance the acidic lemon notes of a fresh goat cheese.

Crunch: Crunch gives our plate texture, while also being a vehicle for cheese. I prefer simple salted crackers, since those with strong seasoning, such as garlic or onion, can overpower the flavor of the cheese. Nuts are a great addition as well, adding a fatty crunch to your bite, or acting as a smooth palate cleanser in between. Always serve That Crunch Plate on the side of your cheese plate—more on that on page 10.

Dip: I love how versatile dips can be. I use them to take the sweetness on the plate up a notch. Adding something like honey or fig jam pairs wonderfully with many cheeses, making for a great contrast to the salty notes. Or if I'm in a savory mood, I play with the tangy elements on the plate, pairing a grainy mustard with an aged cheddar, for example.

Garnish: Finally, don't forget to garnish! Fresh herbs and edible flowers can be the final beautiful detail on your cheese plate creation. I love incorporating a garnish into the bite itself. For example, I'll use fresh basil on a plate with mozzarella and tomato, or add some mint if I'm working with feta and fruit. The garnish also puts that final aesthetic touch on a cheese plate, elevating it to achieve that visual "wow" factor.

that crunch plate

You might notice that many of these plates don't feature many crackers or slices of bread. I want to save the precious cheese plate real estate for big flavors and colorful pairings, so I like to serve That Crunch Plate on the side of every cheese plate. This is your refillable sidekick for crunchy cheese vehicles like flatbread crackers, fruit and nut crisps, water crackers, French bread, baguettes, focaccia, ciabatta, and more. Add a few garnishes of fresh herbs or edible flowers to your cracker plate for a fun little pop of color.

party themes and music

When throwing a party, it's important to set a theme and an intention. Themes can be anything from a birthday celebration to a beach picnic, from a cozy fireside supper to a bachelorette party. It can be about celebrating an actual holiday, or just a general mood—remember, a party is a mindset. Setting a theme lets you tell a story through your cheese plate creation's flavors and colors. I also love to match music to my party theme. Like a good cheese plate, a party ignites the senses, and music is key in setting an overall mood. I'm the type of person who has music playing 24/7, always envisioning my life like a movie with a soundtrack, and you should do the same with parties. Some of my favorite memories are cheese parties that turn into full-blown dance parties, with me singing Whitney Houston's "I Want to Dance with Somebody" while chomping on a slice of Comté. Even if the party consists of just you, taking a break from the workday with That Elevated Desk Lunch Plate (page 90), you can blast some of your favorite tunes and transport yourself. I love how both music and cheese have a different style for every mood, making you feel all the emotions of being alive.

that cheese playlist

Each cheese plate in this book has a musical playlist to accompany it. Scan the QR code below and find the plate you're making. Press play and enjoy an all-around sensory experience to set the vibe.

tablescapes and that cheese palette

When I'm planning a party, I like to use the cheese plate as the actual vision board to inspire the mood and aesthetics. Throughout this book you'll find four-color cheese palettes. These are four colors featured on the cheese plate that can influence the details of your party. Turn to page 14 for a few examples! Once I have my palette established, I start thinking about the tablescape, which contributes to the style and setting of the gathering. Start with the very basics: the table. Consider the size and purpose of your party. Is this a seated dinner party, or a mingle-and-graze soiree? If you're planning for your guests to be seated, create individual place settings, with the cheese board as your fabulous centerpiece. A place setting should include a plate, napkin, glassware, and utensils. Feel free to get creative when it comes to plate and napkin colors. However, it's nice to make sure the table isn't overcrowded with color and detail so the cheese plate can shine as the center of attention. Once you have the cheese plate and serving utensils down, fill in the empty spaces with flowers, candles, and greenery. You can layer greens down the center of the table for an organic table runner or make multiple flower arrangements to display across the table. Tea light candles or simple candlesticks work great for glowy, ambient lighting.

Always have an array of cheese knives, tongs, spoons, and forks to make serving your cheese plate creations simple and sanitary for your guests.

The many types of cheese knives out there can be intimidating, but I narrowed them down to my four essentials.

Fork-Tipped Spear: This knife allows you to slice into semi-hard cheeses, then use the tip to pick up the slice with ease.

Flat-Head Knife: This is a great knife to cut soft cheese like brie or camembert. The surface area makes for clean, easy cuts.

Soft-Cheese Spreader: This knife is perfect for soft, spreadable cheeses like soft-ripened goat, creamy blue, and burrata.

Spade Knife: This knife is the best for cutting into hard cheeses, like Parmigiano-Reggiano or Grana Padano. The sharp tip breaks through the cheese well. This can also work for making sharp cheddar "rustic crumbles." Insert the knife vertically into the cheese and twist with your wrist to break off uneven cubes for serving.

cheese plate essentials

cheese characteristics

The world of cheese knows no bounds. There are cheeses made with cow's milk, goat's milk, sheep's milk, buffalo milk, and mixed milk (a blend of different milks), as well as plant-based cheese, which is often made from nuts. Cheese can be categorized as fresh, soft, bloomy, blue, semihard, and hard. Cheese also has a variety of rinds (that's what we call the outer layer)—natural, bloomy, or washed—and sometimes you'll even find cheese wrapped in wax or spruce bark. Now that you know the basics, imagine you're at a party. Someone asks you why you like aged gouda. You know how it tastes, but how do milk styles and textures influence the flavor of the cheese, and how can you describe those flavor notes? This handy infographic can help!

FRESH

smooth, fluffy, soft, moist, spreadable, chalky

COW'S MILK
Mozzarella, Burrata, Cream Cheese
Farmer's Cheese, Paneer, Ricotta,
Mascarpone, Crème Fraîche

LOOK FOR:
mild, buttery, milky, fresh

GOAT'S MILK
Chèvre, Labneh

LOOK FOR:
tangy, milky, floral, lemony, zesty, mild

BRINED SALTED

tender, springy, squeaky, smooth, moist

COW'S MILK
Queso Fresco,
Cheese Curds,
Cotija

LOOK FOR:
salty, creamy,
tangy, milky

SHEEP'S MILK
Feta, Marinated
Sheep/Goat Cheese

LOOK FOR:
salty, creamy,
buttery, thick,
tangy

MIXED MILK
Halloumi

LOOK FOR:
salty, rich,
milky, creamy

BLOOMY

spreadable, creamy, tangy, milky

COW'S MILK
Brie, Camembert, Triple Crème,
Delice de Bourgogne, Harbison,
Rush Creek Reserve, Mt. Tam

LOOK FOR:
buttery, milky, earthy,
barnyard, grassy,
mushroomy

GOAT'S MILK
Soft-ripened Goat, Ash-ripened
Goat, Humboldt Fog, Valençay,
Coupole, Goat Brie, Selles-sur-Cher,
Bûcheron

LOOK FOR:
mild, tangy, milky, buttery,
grassy, salty, herbaceous

MIXED MILK
La Tur, Robiola

LOOK FOR:
mild, buttery, slightly sweet,
yeasty, mushroomy

BLUE

soft, smooth, crumbly, creamy, buttery

COW'S MILK
Stilton, Gorgonzola, Bay Blue, Bayley Hazen Blue,
Rogue River Blue, Huntsman, Red Rock

LOOK FOR:
Pungent, bold, tangy, sweet, funky, peppery

SHEEP'S MILK
Roquefort, Ewe's Blue

LOOK FOR:
rich, sweet cream, velvety, salty, spicy

that cheese flavor flow chart

WASHED RIND

Soft, semi-soft, spreadable, supple, sticky exterior, dense

COW'S MILK

Taleggio, Époisses, Maroilles, Muenster, Stinking Bishop, Limburger, Morbier

LOOK FOR:

pungent, funky, barnyard smell, mild taste, fruity, mushroomy, creamy

SEMI-HARD

supple, waxy, smooth, shiny, thick

COW'S MILK

Havarti, Fontina, Young Gouda, Colby Jack, Emmentaler, Asiago, Mahón, Bellavitano

LOOK FOR:

plush, creamy, mild, buttery, mildly fruity, nutty, grassy

GOAT'S MILK

Drunken Goat, Goat Cheddar, Young Goat Gouda

LOOK FOR:

mild, smooth, gentle, mildly fruity, tangy, herbaceous

SHEEP'S MILK

Queso Roncal, Young Pecorino, Young Manchego

LOOK FOR:

tangy, wooly, herbaceous, milky, slightly sweet

HARD

dense, thick, crumbly, flakey, crunchy, rustic

COW'S MILK

Parmigiano Reggiano, Gruyère, Comté, Aged Cheddar, Aged Gouda, Grana Padano, Tomme, Mimolette

LOOK FOR:

bold, sharp, nutty, grassy, piquant, toasted, earthy, slightly sweet

GOAT'S MILK

Aged Goat Gouda, Garrotxa, Aged Goat Cheddar

LOOK FOR:

rich, savory, tangy, caramel, earthy, nutty

SHEEP'S MILK

Aged Manchego, Pecorino Romano, Ossau-Iraty, Fiore Sardo

LOOK FOR:

savory, slightly sweet, nutty, sharp, zesty

cheese pairings

Throughout this book you'll find **"bite builders"** for each plate, which are my personal favorite flavor combinations on the board. While pairings are always personal, the ultimate goal is to create something that tastes even more delicious than the individual parts. You can mix and match any way you'd like though—in fact, I encourage you to play with your food! I like to think about the scene in one of my favorite movies, *Ratatouille,* where you see fireworks exploding in Remy's mind when he tastes cheese and strawberries together. That's what we're going for! Here are some handy tips for out-of-the-box pairings.

Find Your Opposite: I love to create contrast in flavor and textures. Pairing a stinky blue with a sweet honey or a harder aged Manchego with a soft dried apricot creates a unique bite with dimension.

Flavor Note Friendship: Think about the specific flavor notes you like in each cheese, and pair that with something that has a similar vibe. For example, smoked cheddar has a robust savory quality that Genoa salami shares.

Memories and Musings: Is there a food pairing that reminds you of a childhood memory or favorite meal? For example, I used to love strawberry cheesecake as a kid. I like to create the perfect homage to that dessert by using fresh goat cheese, strawberries, and a drizzle of honey on a shortbread cookie.

What Grows Together Goes Together: This phrase is commonly used in wine pairings to match food and wine from the same part of the world, but it also works for cheese! Items from the same geographic region come from a similar terroir (a cheese's natural environment). If people have been eating certain foods together as part of their national cuisine, you've probably got a good match. For example, Parmigiano-Reggiano pairs beautifully with prosciutto di Parma since both are from Parma, Italy.

Cheese Your Own Adventure: Don't be afraid to get creative and have fun with your pairings! Start with a cheese and check the chart on page 22. Consider the base flavor notes and add . . .

1 or 2 flavors: sweet, salty, bitter, sour, umami (savory)
1 or 2 textures: juicy, crunchy, jammy, smooth, crisp

For example, on That Cheese Date Plate, you can make a bite with Italian truffle cheese, prosciutto, and strawberry champagne jam. The truffle cheese is our base, with a savory flavor and smooth texture. The prosciutto is the salty element, while the jam adds a touch of sweetness. A match made in heaven!

simple styling

Flavor is the most important element when crafting a cheese plate for a party, but aesthetics can also play a big role. The way you cut and style your cheese and meat can create stunning detail, as well as making for easy serving. It's important to consider the age of your cheese while slicing and dicing. Hard, crumbly cheese like parmesan won't hold up in thick triangular wedges, while a fresh goat cheese will be nearly impossible to arrange in even cubes.

If you follow only one rule, make it this one: always precut hard cheeses for easy grazing. It's always heartbreaking when you see a huge block of cheddar on the table at a party with no way of cutting into it. Making sure it's easy for your guests to serve themselves lets everyone focus their energy on flavors, pairings, and conver-

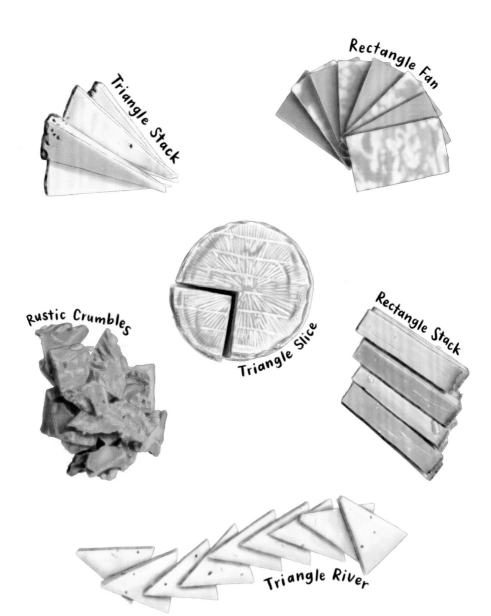

Triangle Stack

Rectangle Fan

Rustic Crumbles

Triangle Slice

Rectangle Stack

Triangle River

sation. I prefer to use a large sharp chef's knife for precutting my cheese, then using cheese knives for serving. For a softer cheese like brie, I typically use a long, thin prep knife (specifically for soft cheese) or a cheese wire. For charcuterie, prosciutto looks best folded in ribbons and is easiest to style while cold, whereas salami works well folded in quarters and is easiest to style while at room temperature. Even the way you decide to slice your produce helps with flavor pairings and color schemes. To the left are my favorite ways to style cheese!

plates and ramekins

The foundation of any cheese plate is the actual plate itself, along with any small jars or ramekins to hold jams and briny items. I use the term plate generally, but this can refer to a board, platter, slate, shallow bowl—pretty much any flat surface. Mix and match with whatever is in your kitchen when crafting a beautiful spread for a party!

serving sizes

I'm often asked, "How many people does this plate serve?" Although there's no exact way to predict your guests' appetite, I added an estimated serving size for each plate in the book, based on the fact that these will be served as appetizers. Remember, though, that the occasion is an important predictor of serving size. Is it a girls' night in, where the plate is the focus of the evening? Or is it a graduation party, where the cheese plate shares the spotlight with other dishes? See the next page for some exact serving sizes according to cheesemongers, whether you're looking at a starter or main course.

CHEESE:

Appetizer—3 ounces per person

Entree—6 ounces per person

MEAT:

Appetizer—1 ounce per person

Entree—2 ounces per person

PRODUCE:

Appetizer—3 ounces per person

Entree—4 ounces per person

CRUNCH:

Appetizer—4 to 6 crackers per person

Entree—8 to 10 crackers per person

DIP:

Appetizer—½ ounce per person

Entree—1 ounce per person

storing tips

To store leftover cheese (a rare occurrence if you're anything like me and my friends), try to stay away from plastic wrap. This causes excess condensation and tends to suffocate the cheese, which actually needs to breathe in the fridge. Parchment paper, beeswax paper, and cheese paper can ensure the freshness of your leftovers.

If you build a cheese plate but want to store it before serving, remove dry items like nuts and crackers before placing the whole thing in the refrigerator. If you're storing it for less than twelve hours, I'll allow plastic wrap to cover the whole plate. For storage longer than twelve hours, take your plate apart and individually wrap each item, then reconstruct it closer to party time.

1

MOOD BOARDS

Setting an overall mood for your gathering can help dictate the details. If you're picturing an intimate moment,

something as simple as soothing lighting, soft music, and delicate flowers can transform even the starkest space. This chapter highlights the plates that evoke a feeling or memory and engage the senses. Mood boards act as wonderful conversation starters. That First Sip of Coffee Plate can ignite the feeling of waking up to a beautiful breakfast spread. Maybe a mood board reminds you of gathering with your family on a holiday or savoring a moment of peace on vacation. I like to see these plates as the gateway to deeper connection by igniting the senses in real time.

When building a cheese plate mood board, you also want to consider color theme. By tying in colors on the plate with details on the table, your guests will be drawn into a full sensory experience. For each plate, I will suggest a scheme of colors to plan your party around. For example, That By the Fire Plate consists of mainly red, brown, and beige colors. Try leaning into this earthy theme by serving your board on a rustic table, accompanied by winter greens next to a fireplace. And remember: At the end of the day, the most important thing is expressing your own creativity and showcasing your personal party vision.

that WARM TONES *plate*

Colors play an important role in setting a theme. On this plate, feel the warmth of red, pink, and orange hues. This board reminds me of a gathering at sunset, with the colors intensifying as the sun dips below the horizon. Here we have two French cheeses, a creamy and earthy camembert and a nutty, bold Comté. I also include an aged cheddar with a zing of sharpness and Italian dry salami to complement the savory notes. To finish it off, sweet seasonal produce creates a bold color palette with juicy pairings.

The Plate: ROUND PORCELAIN PLATE, 14-INCH DIAMETER • SERVES 5 TO 6

1—CHEESE
Camembert
Comté
Sweet red cheddar

2—MEAT
Italian dry salami

3—PRODUCE
Dried clementines

Dried apricots
Dried papaya
Strawberries
Peaches
Raspberries

4—CRUNCH
Honey sesame
almonds
Focaccia

5—DIP
Raspberry jam
Honeycomb

6—GARNISH
Dried edible flowers

Bite Builder

- Camembert + peaches + honeycomb: *Creamy, juicy, and sweet*
- Comté + salami + raspberry jam: *Nutty, savory, and sweet*
- Sweet red cheddar + dried apricots + honey sesame almonds: *Sharp, sweet, and crunchy*
- Sweet red cheddar + salami + dried papaya: *Sharp, savory, and sweet*

- **TCP's favorite Comté / Comté styles:** *Comté Saint Antoine, Alp Blossom, Pleasant Ridge Reserve*

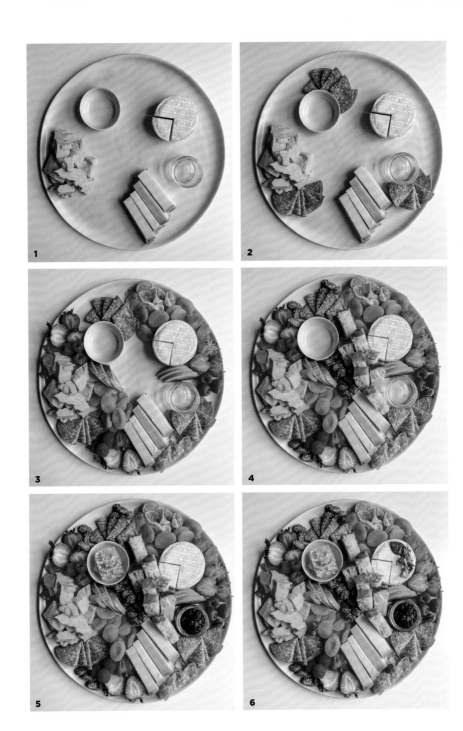

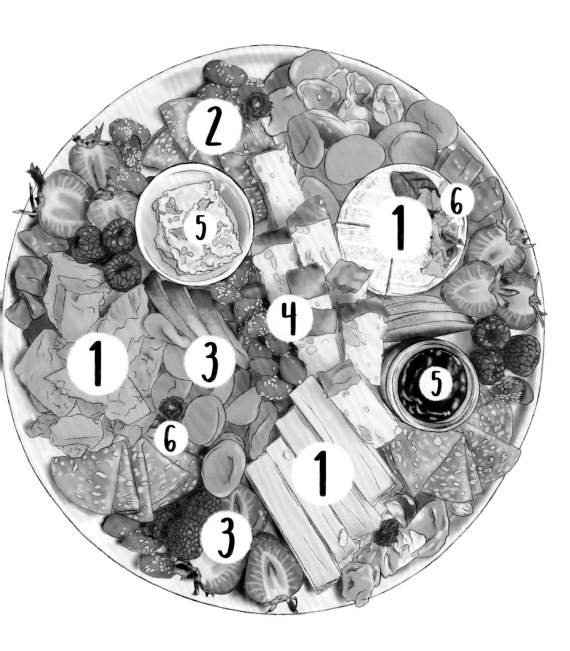

that COOL TONES *plate*

The deep blue and purple hues on this plate set a mood that feels calming and peaceful, like a simple get together by a lake or ocean. Sit back, take a deep breath, and relax. These soothing shades are complemented by pungent and bright pairings, like a stinky aged blue and a tangy blueberry goat cheese. Both cheeses pair well with sweet accompaniments, like dark-chocolate-covered almonds, cocoa-dusted cashews, fresh fruit, and a mixed berry jam.

The Plate: ROUND PORCELAIN PLATE, 12-INCH DIAMETER • SERVES 3 TO 4

1—CHEESE
Blue cheese
Blueberry goat cheese

2—MEAT
N/A

3—PRODUCE
Blackberries
Blueberries
Grapes

4—CRUNCH
Blue potato chips
Fruit and nut crackers
Dark-chocolate-covered almonds
Cocoa-dusted cashews

5—DIP
Mixed berry jam

6—GARNISH
Edible violas

Bite Builder

- Blue cheese + grapes + potato chips: ***Pungent, sweet, and salty***
- Blue cheese + blackberries + mixed berry jam: ***Bold, juicy, and sweet***
- Blueberry goat cheese + blueberries + cocoa-dusted cashews: ***Tangy, juicy, and sweet***
- Blueberry goat cheese + dark-chocolate-covered almonds + fruit and nut crackers: ***Creamy, sweet, and crunchy***

- **TCP's favorite blue cheeses:** *Roquefort, Bayley Hazen Blue, Rogue River Blue, Bay Blue*

that FIRST SIP *of* COFFEE *plate*

I love a good brunch board. There's nothing like waking up to the smell of fresh coffee and sizzling maple sausages to jump-start your day. I wanted to embody those joyful morning memories on this plate, with espresso-rubbed cheddar, breakfast brie, and herby chèvre. I always put everything-bagel seasoning on, well, everything, so I whipped that into a dip too. Feel free to serve alongside some fresh bagels for extra crunch.

The Plate: ROUND ENAMEL PLATE, 16-INCH DIAMETER • SERVES 6 TO 7

1—CHEESE
Chèvre with herbs
Espresso-rubbed cheddar
Breakfast brie

2—MEAT
Herby smoked salmon
Maple chicken sausages
Hard-boiled eggs

3—PRODUCE
Cherry tomatoes
Avocado
Cucumbers
Capers
Pickled red onions

4—CRUNCH
Focaccia

5—DIP
Everything Bagel
Seasoned Whipped Feta
(recipe on page 213)

6—GARNISH
Fresh dill

Bite Builder

- Chèvre with herbs + hard-boiled eggs + avocado + pickled red onions: **Creamy, mild, smooth, and tangy**
- Espresso-rubbed cheddar + maple chicken sausages + focaccia: **Sharp, savory, sweet, and buttery**
- Breakfast brie + cherry tomatoes + capers + focaccia: **Buttery, juicy, salty, and crisp**
- Seasoned whipped feta + smoked salmon + cucumbers + pickled red onions: **Tangy, salty, fresh, and zesty**

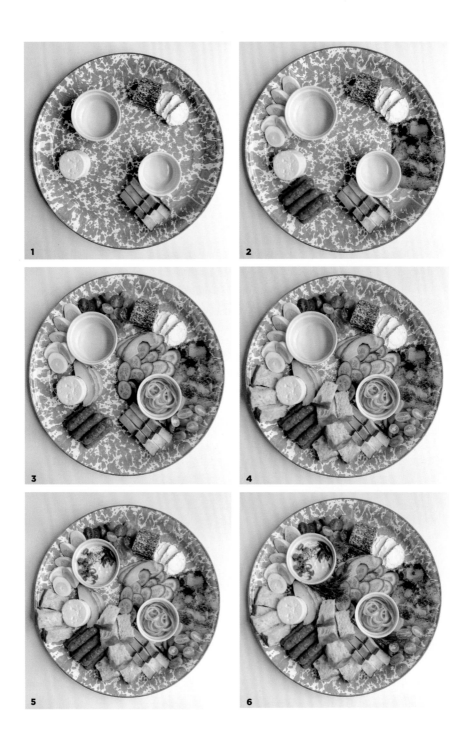

that BY *the* FIRE *plate*

This plate is for those cozy chilly days, when all I want is to curl up next to a fireplace bringing comforting warmth to the room. This creation features a decadent brie brûlée paired with apple-smoked cheddar, truffle gouda, smoky charcuterie, and sweet accompaniments. To make the brie brûlée, top it with a layer of sugar and toast it with a butane torch or place it under the broiler for two to three minutes, until golden brown.

The Plate: RECTANGULAR WOODEN BOARD, 9¹⁄₂ × 13¹⁄₂ INCHES · SERVES 4 TO 5

1—CHEESE
Apple-smoked cheddar
Truffle gouda
Brie brûlée

2—MEAT
Soppressata
Dry coppa

3—PRODUCE
Dried cherries
Dried figs
Raspberries

4—CRUNCH
Fruit and nut crackers
Dark-chocolate-covered almonds
Candied pecans

5—DIP
Honey

6—GARNISH
Fresh rosemary
Fresh thyme

Bite Builder

- Apple-smoked cheddar + dry coppa + dried figs: ***Sharp, savory, and sweet***
- Truffle gouda + soppressata + dried cherries: ***Savory, aromatic, and tangy***
- Brie brûlée + raspberries + dark-chocolate-covered almonds: ***Creamy, juicy, and sweet***
- Brie brûlée + soppressata + honey: ***Creamy, savory, and sweet***

- **TCP's favorite truffle goudas:** *Artikaas Truffle Gouda, Marieke Truffle Gouda*

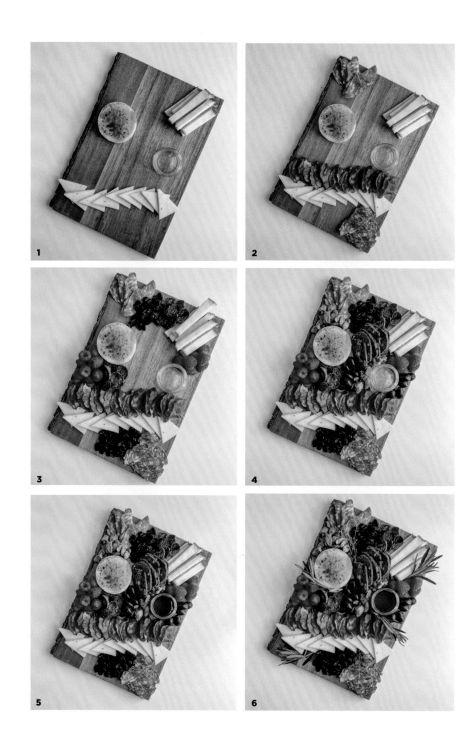

that TIME *for a* MARTINI *plate*

It's happy hour! My favorite cocktail is hands down a martini (with vodka, slightly dirty). Martinis pair wonderfully with cheese, due to their salty nature and briny, zesty garnishes. This plate channels the sound of the cocktail shaker, the feel of the ice-cold glass, and the crispness of that first sip. Even if you don't drink, this plate is full of delicious cheeses and decadent pairings, including feta with cornichons, blue cheese with olives, and tangy Sweety Drop miniature peppers.

The Plate: ROUND SOAPSTONE PLATE, 12-INCH DIAMETER • SERVES 3 TO 4

1—CHEESE
Marinated feta
Blue cheese

2—MEAT
Smoked salami

3—PRODUCE
Roasted red peppers

Cornichons
Spanish Queen olives
Sweety Drop peppers
Pearl onions

4—CRUNCH
Crusty bread
Marcona almonds

5—DIP
Extra-virgin olive oil

6—GARNISH
Fresh sage
Lemon twists

Bite Builder

- Blue cheese + Spanish Queen olives + crusty bread: ***Pungent, sweet, and crisp***
- Blue cheese + salami + Marcona almonds: ***Creamy, savory, sweet, and crunchy***
- Feta + roasted red peppers + crusty bread: ***Salty, sweet, and tangy***
- Feta + Spanish Queen olives + olive oil + crusty bread: ***Briny, salty, and buttery***

that SIGNS *of* SPRING *plate*

Bright green buds pop on the trees and tulips make their way aboveground after a long winter. Spring inches in with brighter days, and it's time to celebrate. This plate is infused with fresh and vibrant flavors, seasonal produce, and savory pairings. The rosemary asiago is an Italian-inspired cow's milk cheese, a cross between a sharp cheddar and a nutty parmesan, with underlying notes of fruit. The marinated sheep and goat cheese on the plate has a smooth, velvety texture to balance out the herby purple potato salad and the fresh marinated cucumbers.

The Plate: RECTANGULAR WOODEN BOARD, 14 × 20 INCHES • SERVES 4 TO 6

1—CHEESE
Marinated sheep and goat cheese with herbs
Rosemary asiago

2—MEAT
Ham

3—PRODUCE
Herby Purple Potato Salad (recipe on page 223)
Marinated cucumbers with red onion, dill, and parsley
Blanched green beans with toasted pine nuts and crispy garlic

4—CRUNCH
French bread
Seeded crackers
Walnuts

5—DIP
Balsamic glaze

6—GARNISH
Fresh dill
Fresh tarragon
Fresh parsley

Bite Builder

- Marinated sheep and goat cheese + marinated cucumbers + balsamic glaze + French bread: ***Creamy, fresh, and sweet***
- Marinated sheep and goat cheese + ham + crackers + dill: ***Tangy, salty, crunchy, and fresh***
- Rosemary asiago + green beans + balsamic glaze: ***Sharp, garlicky, and sweet***
- Rosemary asiago + ham + purple potato salad + walnuts + parsley: ***Nutty, salty, herby, and crunchy***

that GOLDEN HOUR *plate*

I made this plate on a solo trip to the Catskills in upstate New York. I booked an Airbnb in a cabin on a farm, surrounded by wildflowers and rolling hills. Seeking inspiration for this very book, I made my way to the local market and picked up some provisions. It was a golden hour, and the sun peering through the window inspired the colors. I found a delicious local camembert—a soft-ripened cheese with a blend of sheep's milk, cow's milk, and cream—that paired beautifully with a sweet fig jam. The clothbound cheddar brings some bold and sharp flavors to the plate, perfect to stand up against the savory salami or the spicy candied ginger.

The Plate: OVAL PORCELAIN PLATE, 7½ × 12 INCHES • SERVES 3 TO 4

1—CHEESE
Hudson Valley camembert
Clothbound cheddar

2—MEAT
Italian dry salami

3—PRODUCE
Watermelon radishes
Persian cucumbers
Candied ginger

4—CRUNCH
Fruit and nut crackers
Mixed nuts

5—DIP
Fig jam

6—GARNISH
Fresh thyme
Marigolds

Bite Builder

- Camembert + fig jam + fruit and nut crackers: *Creamy, sweet, and crunchy*
- Camembert + cucumbers + mixed nuts: *Buttery, fresh, and salty*
- Clothbound cheddar + candied ginger + fig jam: *Nutty, spicy, and sweet*
- Clothbound cheddar + Italian dry salami + watermelon radishes: *Sharp, savory, and fresh*

- **TCP's favorite clothbound cheddars:** *Cabot Clothbound, Montgomery's Cheddar, Milton Creamery Flory's Truckle*

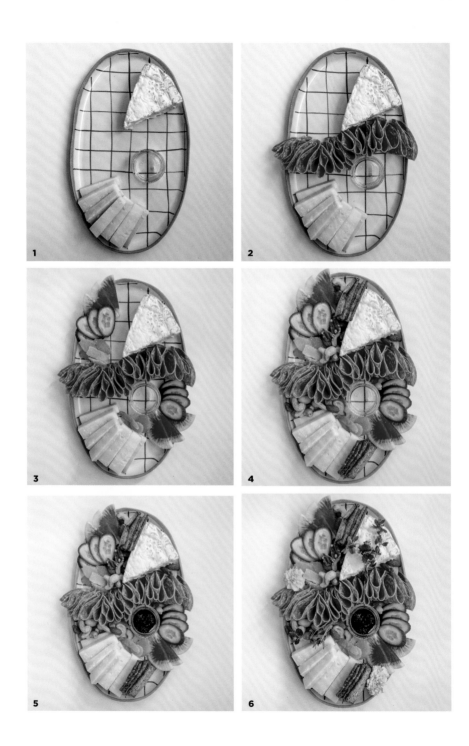

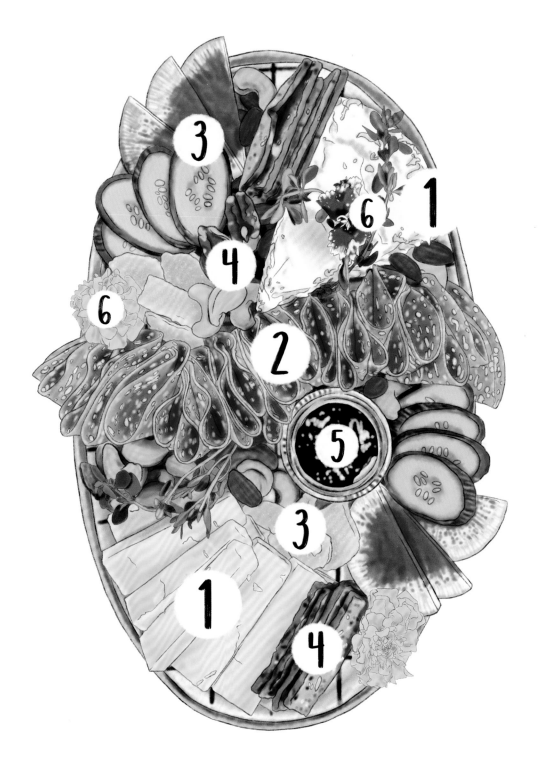

that CHEESE DATE *plate*

If you share a cheese plate on a first date, a second date is not just possible, but likely (I tell you this from personal experience). This plate is decadent, spicy, sweet, and savory—a flirty combination for the taste buds. I wanted to include two luxurious cheeses—a ripe, gooey goat brie and a truffle-dusted Italian cheese called Sottocenere al Tartufo. Make it a hot date with the addition of warm dates stuffed with blue cheese and candied ginger, and this plate is guaranteed to be a good time.

The Plate: ROUND PORCELAIN PLATE, 10½-INCH DIAMETER · SERVES 2 TO 3

1—CHEESE
Goat brie
Sottocenere al Tartufo

2—MEAT
Prosciutto

3—PRODUCE
Raspberries

Warm Stuffed Dates
with Blue Cheese, Speck,
and Candied Ginger
(recipe on page 237)
Dried cherries

4—CRUNCH
Marcona almonds
Cocoa-dusted cashews
Fruit and nut crackers

5—DIP
Strawberry
champagne jam

6—GARNISH
Fresh thyme

Bite Builder

- Goat brie + raspberries + strawberry champagne jam: ***Creamy, juicy, and sweet***
- Goat brie + dried cherries + cocoa-dusted cashews: ***Buttery, tart, and sweet***
- Sottocenere al Tartufo + prosciutto + strawberry champagne jam: ***Earthy, savory, and fruity***
- Sottocenere al Tartufo + prosciutto + Marcona almonds: ***Nutty, salty, and crunchy***

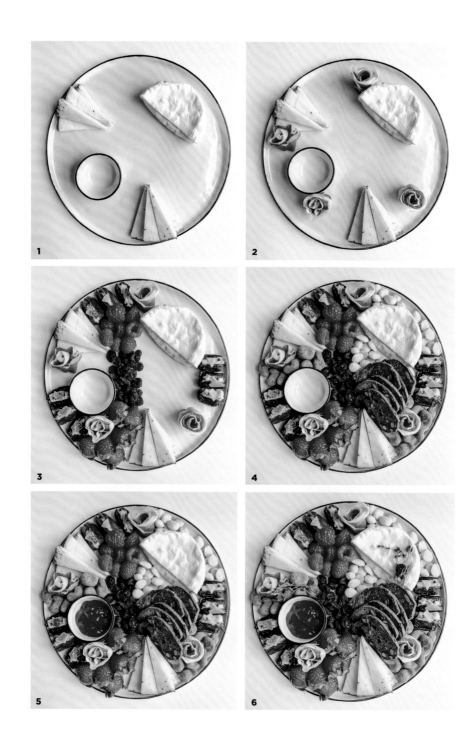

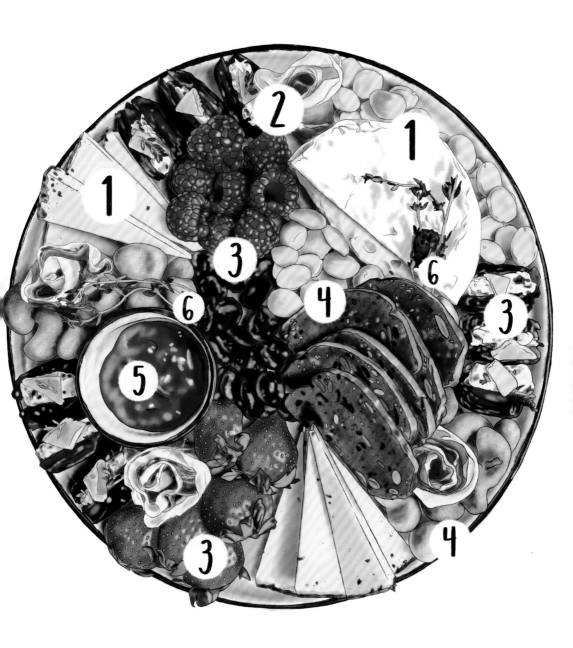

2

CELEBRATE SMALL

My favorite types of parties are the small, intimate ones. I love how they can lead to deeper conversations and real connections,

sometimes with unexpected new friends. The plates in this chapter celebrate the ways in which we can enjoy cheese on a smaller scale. You can curate a plate just for yourself, or share with a loved one. You can make one to take on the road for a lunch to go, or make one as a fun activity with kids.

Small plates encourage you to pay extra attention to pairings and detail. With less space to fill, you can be intentional about your choices of cheese and how they mingle with the accompaniments. Smaller plates have less room for aesthetic creativity, so the flavor pairings stand out with greater importance. While I love a super-sized grazing table, cheese plates do not need to be large and extravagant to be special. A cheese plate's a cheese plate, no matter how small!

that PARTY *for* ONE *plate*

Some of my favorite cheese plates are the ones I've enjoyed all by myself. When building a personal cheese plate, I always like to select my all-time favorite pairings so that every bite is a party. Here, I chose two of my favorite cheeses, an Italian toma and a soft-ripened cow and goat's milk cheese called Cremont. Toma is a cow's milk cheese with a buttery, creamy flavor and slight grassy finish, which pairs great with something savory like prosciutto, while Cremont goes well with something sweet, like dried figs or fresh strawberries.

The Plate: OVAL PORCELAIN PLATE, 6 × 8½ INCHES · SERVES 1

1—CHEESE
Toma
Cremont

2—MEAT
Prosciutto di Parma

3—PRODUCE
Radishes
Strawberries
Dried figs

4—CRUNCH
Marcona almonds
Rustic crisps

5—DIP
Raspberry jam

6—GARNISH
Fresh thyme
Fresh mint

Bite Builder

- Toma + prosciutto + raspberry jam: ***Buttery, savory, and sweet***
- Toma + dried figs + Marcona almonds: ***Grassy, sweet, and crunchy***
- Cremont + strawberries + dried figs: ***Creamy, fresh, and sweet***
- Cremont + prosciutto + radishes: ***Luscious, savory, and fresh***

- **TCP'S favorite mixed-milk cheeses:** *La Tur, Mobay, Hummingbird*

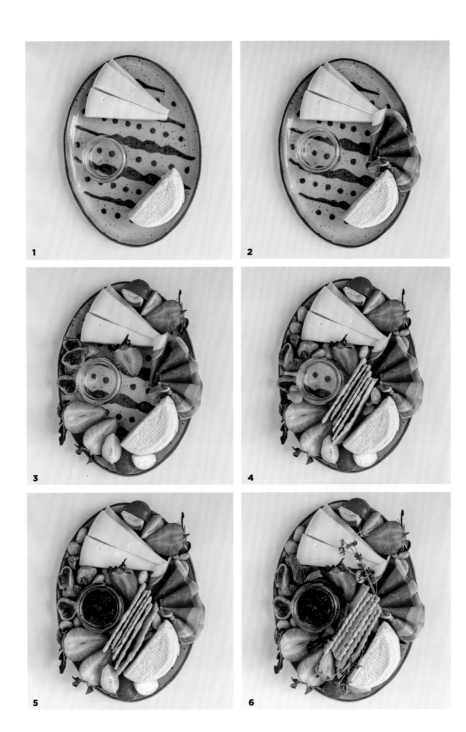

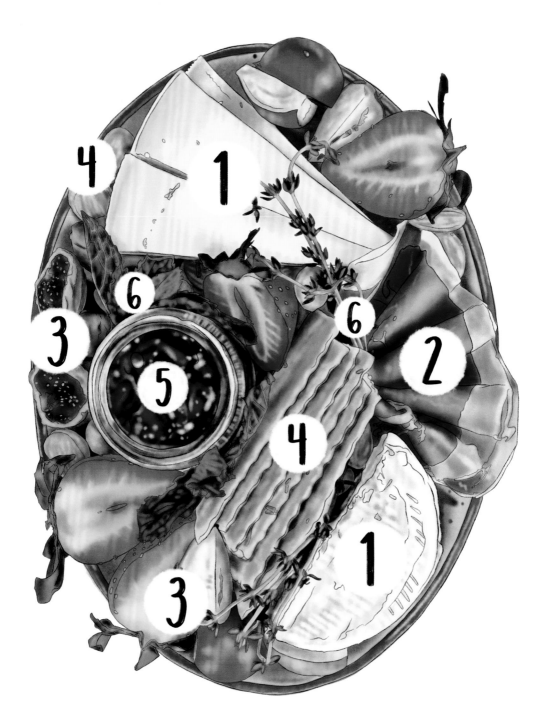

that PERSONAL PICNIC *plate*

Let's celebrate warm weather with a personal picnic outdoors! My ideal picnic menu includes robust cheeses and crunchy crackers. On this plate I paired a smoked cheddar and an aged gouda with a variety of savory accompaniments, like herby olives and fennel salami. Grab a blanket, a nice book, and your cheese plate for a relaxing party of an afternoon.

The Plate: RECTANGULAR GLASS DISH, 5 × 8 INCHES · SERVES 1 TO 2

1—CHEESE
Aged gouda
Smoked cheddar

2—MEAT
Hard fennel salami

3—PRODUCE
Herby assorted olives
Persian cucumbers

4—CRUNCH
Toasted hazelnuts
Rustic crackers
Rice crackers

5—DIP
N/A

6—GARNISH
Flowering basil
Marigolds

Bite Builder

- Smoked cheddar + fennel salami + cucumber: ***Smoky, savory, and fresh***
- Smoked cheddar + herby olives + rice crackers: ***Sharp, salty, and crisp***
- Aged gouda + fennel salami + herby olives: ***Nutty, savory, and briny***
- Aged gouda + hazelnuts + rustic crackers: ***Creamy, savory, and crunchy***

- **TCP's favorite goudas:** *L'Amuse Gouda, Beemster Classic, Ewephoria (sheep's milk gouda)*

that KIDDOS *plate*

It's okay to play with your food! Creative cheese plates are an exciting way to get kids involved in the party. By arranging the food in a colorful and vibrant way, you'll keep any kiddo entertained and encouraged to eat. I also used some funky-shaped vegetable cutters to create cucumber stars, Colby Jack flowers, and strawberry hearts. With mild cheese like mozzarella and kid-friendly snacks like ants on a log and cheesy crackers, this plate is both fun and tasty.

The Plate: RECTANGULAR SECTIONED PLATE, 9 × 10 INCHES • SERVES 2 TO 3

1—CHEESE
Colby Jack
Mini mozzarella balls

2—MEAT
Turkey deli slices
Salami deli slices

3—PRODUCE
Cucumbers
Strawberries
Blueberries
Ants on a log
(celery, almond butter,
dried cranberries)

4—CRUNCH
Cheese crackers
Pretzels

5—DIP
N/A

6—GARNISH
N/A

Bite Builder

- Colby Jack + turkey + pretzels: *Mild, savory, and crunchy*
- Colby Jack + salami + cheese crackers: *Sharp, salty, and cheesy*
- Mozzarella + cucumbers + pretzels: *Creamy, fresh, and crunchy*
- Mozzarella + salami + cheese crackers: *Smooth, salty, and crunchy*

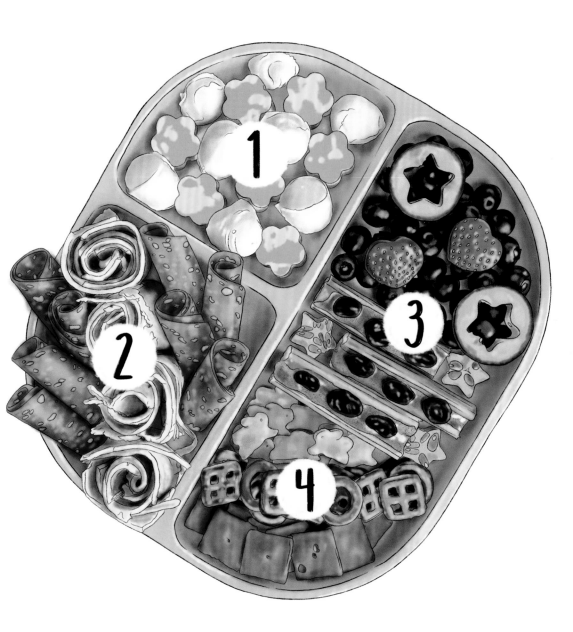

that IN-FLIGHT *plate*

Back in 2019 I accidentally went viral when I built a cheese plate on an airplane tray table. I dubbed this the "In-Flight Cheese Plate Challenge." Over the years, my cheese plates in the sky have become a little more extravagant, and I've befriended every flight attendant I've met. If that's not a party, I don't know what is. This plate is optimized for TSA security, easy to transport and delicious to enjoy on your travels. I chose two hard cheeses that won't become too messy in transit, plus a selection of dried fruit that can last over time. The jam is under the three-ounce limit and the salami is stacked upright to pack it all in! Pro tip: Build your plate in a sectioned tray with a lid so you can pop it in your carry-on with ease. This plate also works for road trips, train journeys, and boat rides!

The Plate: RECTANGULAR SECTIONED TRAY, 6 × 8½ INCHES • SERVES 1 TO 2

1—CHEESE
Emmental
Truffle gouda

2—MEAT
Bresaola
Spicy soppressata

3—PRODUCE
Green grapes
Dried apricots
Dates
Candied ginger

4—CRUNCH
Crackers
Sesame almonds

5—DIP
Fig jam

6—GARNISH
Fresh thyme

Bite Builder

- Emmental + spicy soppressata + dried apricots + crackers: ***Nutty, spicy, sweet, and crunchy***
- Emmental + grapes + fig jam: ***Buttery, juicy, and sweet***
- Truffle gouda + Bresaola + fig jam: ***Robust, savory, and sweet***
- Truffle gouda + dates + sesame almonds: ***Rich, sweet, and crunchy***

- **TCP's favorite Emmental / Emmental styles:** *Emmentaler AOP, Holey Cow, Jarlsberg*

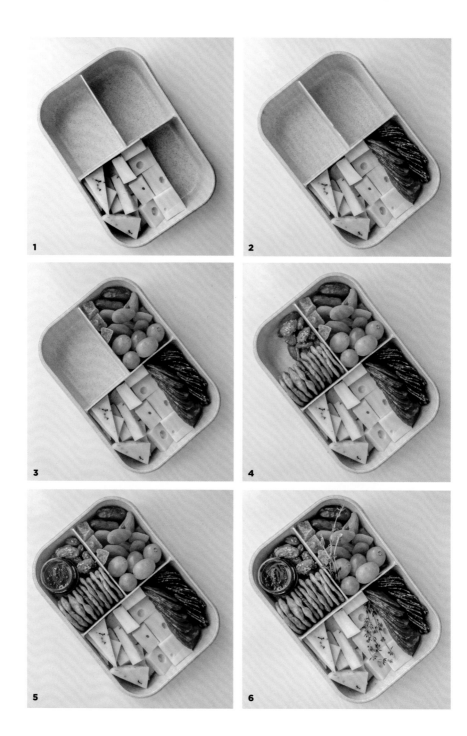

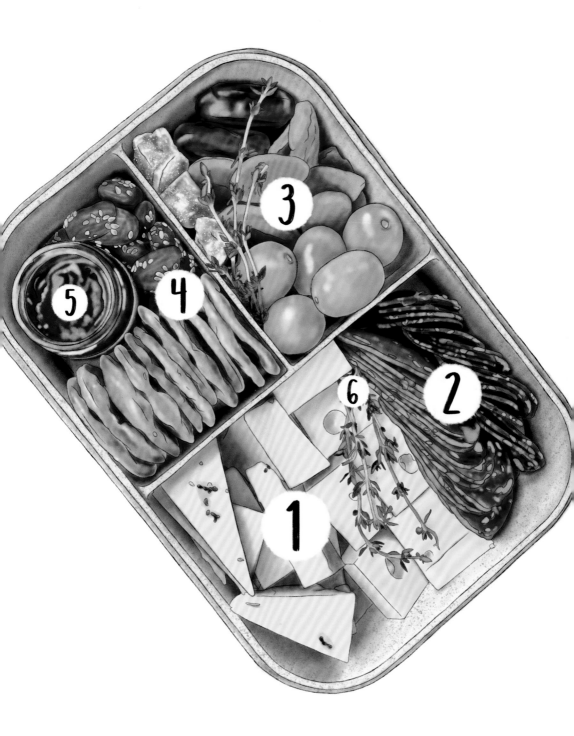

that MEZZE SNACK *bowl*

Any dish loaded with vibrant and herbaceous Mediterranean and Middle Eastern pairings is always a party for your taste buds. This bowl packs in the briny, lemony, and tangy flavor notes with creamy feta, crunchy produce, and smooth hummus. I also added in some takeout chicken shawarma and falafel (support your favorite Middle Eastern restaurant!) for a savory and spicy element, along with colorful beet sauerkraut and warm pita. Enjoy this bowl on its own, or pair with That Colorful Crudités Plate to load up on more fresh veggies!

The Plate: ROUND PORCELAIN BOWL, 9-INCH DIAMETER • SERVES 1 TO 2

1—CHEESE
Feta with herbs

2—MEAT
Chicken shawarma

3—PRODUCE
Persian cucumbers
Beet sauerkraut
Yellow grape tomatoes

4—CRUNCH
Falafel
Warm pita

5—DIP
Hummus
Tahini drizzle

6—GARNISH
Fresh parsley
Fresh dill

Bite Builder

- Feta + chicken shawarma + tomatoes + pita: ***Creamy, savory, juicy, and crisp***
- Feta + falafel + cucumbers + tahini: ***Smooth, rich, fresh, and nutty***
- Feta + hummus + beet sauerkraut: ***Briny, creamy, and bitter***
- Feta + falafel + hummus + cucumbers + tomatoes: ***Rich, savory, smooth, fresh, and juicy***

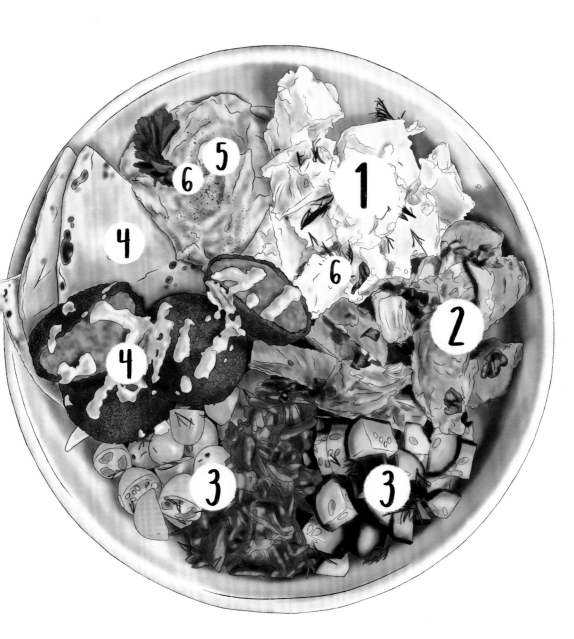

that ELEVATED DESK LUNCH *plate*

This is my favorite weekday lunchtime snack, easy to take with you to the office or enjoy at your work-from-home setup. Think: deconstructed chicken salad sandwich. Dare I say these flavors could make work into a party? The sharp cheddar adds a nice piquant element, while the grapes bring a touch of sweetness to the chicken salad. Taking a moment out of your workday to appreciate your lunch makes for a simple act of mindfulness. No more sad desk lunches!

The Plate: ROUND PORCELAIN PLATE, 10½-INCH DIAMETER • SERVES 1 TO 2

1—CHEESE
Sharp cheddar
Manchego

2—MEAT
Waldorf chicken salad

3—PRODUCE
Celery
Persian cucumbers
Green grapes

4—CRUNCH
Potato chips
Snack-size Italian
bruschetta toasts
Walnuts

5—DIP
Balsamic glaze

6—GARNISH
Fresh chives
Fresh thyme

Bite Builder

- Sharp cheddar + chicken salad + celery + potato chips: ***Sharp, savory, crunchy, and salty***
- Sharp cheddar + grapes + balsamic glaze + bruschetta toasts: ***Sharp, juicy, sweet, and crispy***
- Manchego + chicken salad + cucumbers + balsamic glaze + potato chips: ***Tangy, savory, fresh, sweet, and crispy***
- Manchego + grapes + balsamic glaze + bruschetta toasts: ***Tangy, fresh, fruity, and crispy***

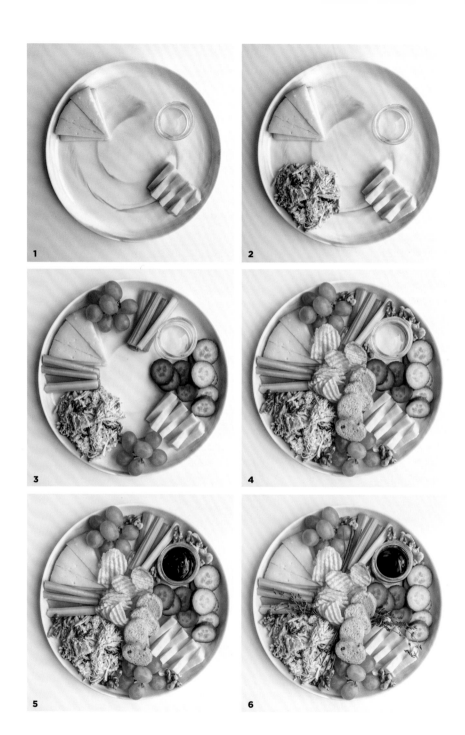

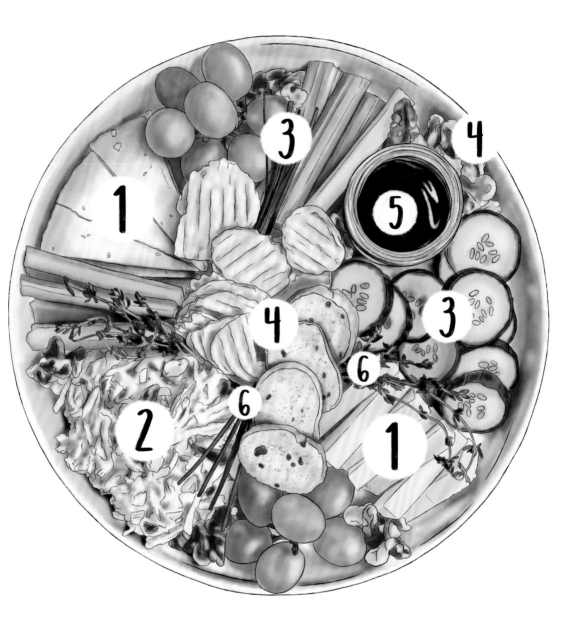

that WINE DOWN *plate*

I love that first sip of wine after a long day of work. It's a little "treat yourself" time, transitioning to a relaxing mood that carries you into the night. This plate channels that energy through sweet and savory pairings like chocolate-covered almonds with a mild, buttery petite camembert. I also added an herbaceous and rich wine-soaked goat's milk cheese from Spain. This plate celebrates the act of slowing down, savoring the moment, and disconnecting from a long day.

The Plate: MARBLE PLATTER, 8 × 8 INCHES · SERVES 1 TO 2

1—CHEESE
Wine-soaked goat cheese
Petite camembert

Dried figs
Strawberries
Raspberries

5—DIP
Cranberry cherry
cabernet jam

2—MEAT
Black pepper hard salami

4—CRUNCH
Chocolate-covered
almonds
Honey sesame almonds
Tea biscuits

6—GARNISH
Fresh rosemary
Dried edible flowers

3—PRODUCE
Dried cherries
Dried raspberries

Bite Builder

- Wine-soaked goat cheese + black pepper hard salami + cranberry cherry cabernet jam: ***Rich, savory, and sweet***
- Wine-soaked goat cheese + dried cherries + chocolate-covered almonds: ***Delicate, tart, and sweet***
- Petite camembert + strawberries + cranberry cherry cabernet jam: ***Creamy, juicy, and sweet***
- Petite camembert + black pepper hard salami + honey sesame almonds: ***Buttery, savory, spicy, and sweet***

- **TCP's favorite wine-soaked cheeses:** *Murcia al Vino (goat's milk), Merlot BellaVitano (cow's milk), Creamy Syrah Toscano (cow's milk)*

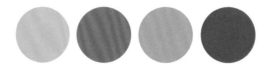

that HERBY FETA *bowl*

At parties, I love serving multiple dishes alongside my cheese plates to complement the entire tablescape. This herby feta bowl is fresh, zesty, and flavorful. The briny feta meets the savory elements of the balsamic marinated grilled chicken, while the fresh produce adds a refreshing crunch. Mix it all together and enjoy! I'd suggest adding this to your tablescape with That Funky Luncheon Plate or That Signs of Spring Plate as a fun, fresh salad.

The Plate: ROUND PORCELAIN BOWL, 9-INCH DIAMETER • SERVES 1 TO 2

1—CHEESE
Feta

2—MEAT
Balsamic grilled
chicken

3—PRODUCE
Cucumbers
Grape tomatoes
Pickled red onions
Castelvetrano olives

4—CRUNCH
Orzo

5—DIP
Green goddess dressing

6—GARNISH
Fresh dill
Lemon wedge
Salt and pepper

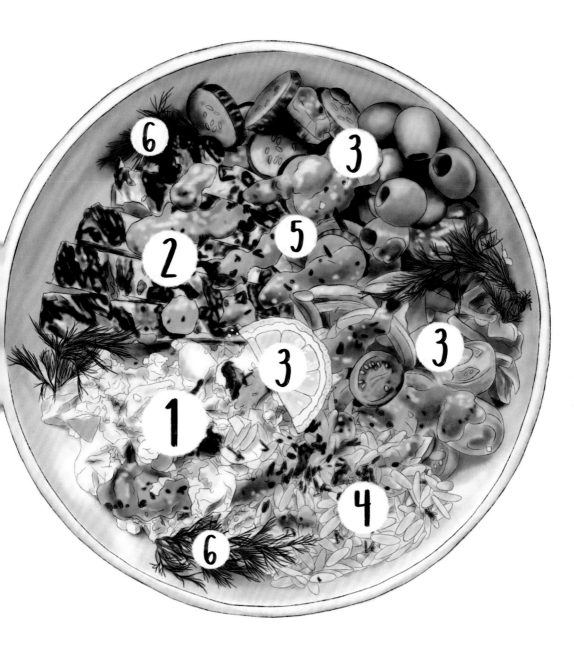

3

GARDEN PARTIES

Though I'm a city girl, I've come to appreciate the great outdoors more and more. Whether it's the first day of summer or the dead of winter, the environment always plays a part in my cheese plate creations. I find nature healing and extremely important for my mental health. NYC living means spending a lot of time indoors or surrounded by buildings and people. When driving to the woods or getting away to the beach, I instantly feel my energy shift. There's nothing on a screen that can replicate the feeling of a sunset, the smell of a forest, or the sound of waves. Every single element on a cheese plate also ties into nature, from the cows whose milk made the cheese itself, to the fresh vegetables and herbs that grow from the ground. I love seeking out local cheese to support farmers in the community, as well as seasonal produce for maximum freshness. This chapter also features a wide variety of vegetarian plates for those who choose not to eat meat. However, some cheeses are not *fully* vegetarian, so depending on how strict you are with your dietary practices, make sure you check ahead of time. Cheeses often use an animal rennet (coagulating enzyme) in the cheese-making process, but there are many different cheeses that use a vegetarian rennet instead. Check the label or ask your local cheesemonger to confirm! Plant-based cheeses can make for an easy swap for many of these plates as well—my favorites are cashew-based cheeses.

When throwing an outdoor gathering, I always love to load up on the floral arrangements. My mom is an avid gardener, and I try to spend time in her backyard as much as I can in the summer. I love to wander around, marveling at her colorful pots and smelling the sweet fragrances. Tying in the colors on a cheese plate with the flower arrangements on the table sets a cohesive mood for the entire gathering.

Ellen Mullen's Flower-Arranging Tips

- *Choose a Variety:* Similar to selecting different cheeses for your plate, presenting a range of flowers lets you feature different textures and colors. Pick three to five different flower types to begin.
- *Add Height:* Floral arrangements are meant to stand out, so adding stalks of different heights creates dimension. You can place taller "statement" flowers toward the middle or on the outskirts for more width.
- *Use Greenery:* A nice way to add color and texture is by filling in the open gaps with different greens, such as ruscus, myrtle, fern, and olive branches.
- *Vase and Place:* Your flower vase is very important to an arrangement as it adds additional style and tone for your gathering. Go with something simple like glass to make the flowers pop, or switch it up with a funky-shaped vase to set your creation apart.
- *Get Creative:* Look at the colors on your cheese plate. Which flowers will complement those hues? Try something outside your comfort zone. Ditch the roses and mix it up with some dahlias! Get some wild green eucalyptus to grow out of the creation in different directions. Let loose and have fun with it. Just like cheese plates, getting creative with flower arranging is a form of self-care.

that APERITIVO *plate*

The Italian act of aperitivo is a cultural ritual. The tradition means "to open" the stomach after work and before dinner, accompanied by a low-alcohol beverage like a spritz or a mixed drink. Aperitivo fare makes for a quintessential light cheese plate. Cheese, olives, and bread are typically enjoyed while decompressing after the day. Sounds like my dream! On this plate, I made a salad with a creamy and velvety buffalo mozzarella, Castelvetrano olives, cucumbers, and tomatoes, then surrounded it with marinated artichokes, fresh melon with basil, taralli crackers, and fresh baked bread with garlic. *Cin-cin!*

The Plate: RECTANGULAR WOODEN BOARD, 12 × 13 INCHES • SERVES 2 TO 3

1—CHEESE
Buffalo Mozzarella Caprese
(recipe on page 229)

2—MEAT
N/A

3—PRODUCE
Cantaloupe
Marinated artichokes
Red radishes
Castelvetrano olives

4—CRUNCH
Italian bread with olives
Fennel taralli crackers

5—DIP
Extra-virgin olive oil with
balsamic vinegar

6—GARNISH
Fresh basil

Bite Builder

- Buffalo Mozzarella Caprese + marinated artichokes + bread: ***Creamy, briny, and crisp***
- Buffalo Mozzarella Caprese + radishes + bread: ***Smooth, sweet, and crunchy***
- Cantaloupe + fennel taralli crackers: ***Sweet and crunchy***
- Bread + olive oil: ***A classic!***

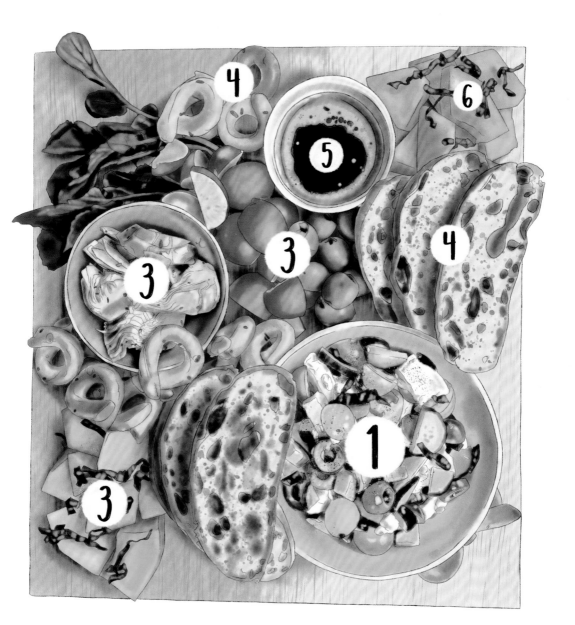

that MUSHROOM MEDLEY *plate*

This plate transports me to a dinner party in the wintertime. There's a chill to the air, the cable-knit sweaters come out of hibernation, and maybe there's a warm fire nearby. There's something so comforting about creamy brie with warm cooked vegetables. Many styles of brie and camembert have subtle mushroom notes. I love mushrooms in all forms, especially when they're crispy and coated in melty cheese. Searing mushrooms transforms the rather subtle vegetable into a savory delicacy that highlights the notes of the brie itself. Pair with a crisp baguette and savory caramelized onion jam for a cozy night.

The Plate: SQUARE SLATE PLATE, 12 × 12 INCHES • SERVES 3 TO 4

1—CHEESE
Brie with mushrooms
Grana Padano

2—MEAT
N/A

3—PRODUCE
Seared Crispy Mushrooms
with Grana Padano
(recipe on page 225)
Marinated assorted olives
Roasted rainbow carrots

4—CRUNCH
French baguette
Dijon pistachios

5—DIP
Caramelized onion jam

6—GARNISH
Fresh thyme

Bite Builder

- Brie with mushrooms + crispy mushrooms + caramelized onion jam + baguette: *Rich, savory, and sweet*
- Brie with mushrooms + roasted carrots + baguette: *Creamy, sweet, and crunchy*
- Grana Padano + crispy mushrooms + baguette: *Sharp, umami, and crunchy*
- Grana Padano + olives + caramelized onion jam + baguette: *Robust, salty, sweet, and crunchy*

- **TCP's favorite brie-style cheeses:** *Brie de Meaux PDO, Melinda Mae, Moses Sleeper, Brie Fermier*

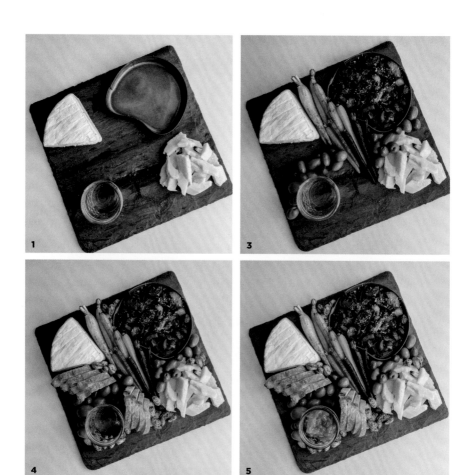

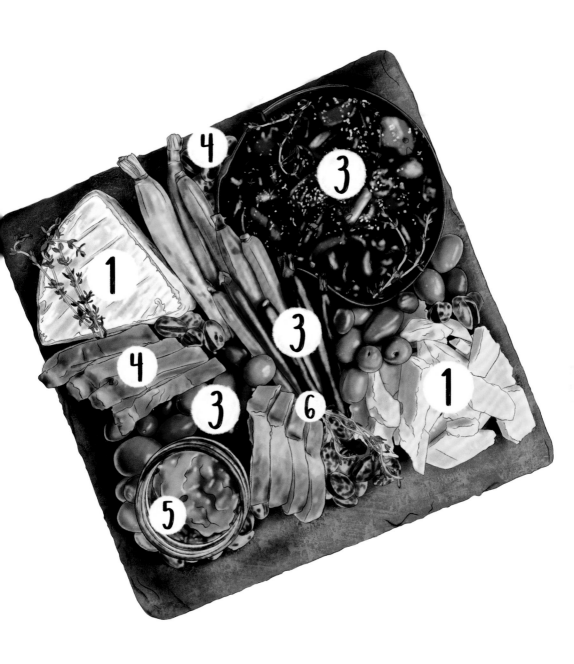

that COLORFUL CRUDITÉS *plate*

This elevated crudités plate channels warm summer days, a refreshing breeze, outdoor gatherings, and great conversation. Thick and creamy labneh mingles with chili onion crisp for a bit of a kick, and sautéed garlicky Broccolini pairs with an herby tahini dip. Be ready to impress your guests while I let you in on a secret: all of the items on this plate are from Trader Joe's.

The Plate: ROUND CERAMIC PLATE, 15½-INCH DIAMETER • SERVES 4 TO 5

1—CHEESE
Labneh (or Greek yogurt)

2—MEAT
N/A

3—PRODUCE
Persian cucumbers
Radishes

Blanched colored
cauliflower
Sautéed Broccolini
with garlic
Celery

4—CRUNCH
Pita crackers
Seeded crackers

5—DIP
Tahini herb dip
Chili onion crisp

6—GARNISH
Fresh dill

Bite Builder

- Labneh + cucumber + pita crackers: ***Creamy, fresh, and crunchy***
- Labneh + sautéed Broccolini + seeded crackers: ***Creamy, garlicky, and crunchy***
- Tahini herb dip + cucumbers + radishes: ***Herby, fresh, and crunchy***
- Tahini herb dip + labneh + celery: ***Herby, creamy, fresh, and crunchy***

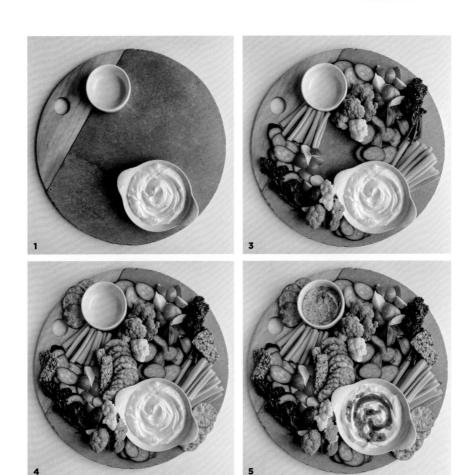

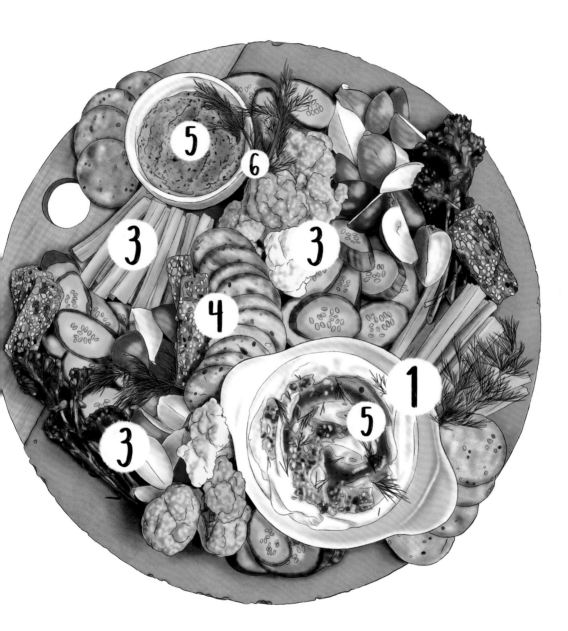

that FUNKY LUNCHEON *plate*

Time to get groovy with it. The colors of this plate were inspired by a cheese called Huntsman, a striped cheddar and blue wedge that is meant to stand out. I tied in the cheddar notes with dried apricots and sweet mixed berry jam, and added fresh mozzarella to be enjoyed alongside crisp cucumbers or atop a toasted crostini. Check out page 15 for a funky tablescape to match!

The Plate: ROUND PORCELAIN PLATE, 12-INCH DIAMETER • SERVES 3 TO 4

1—CHEESE
Huntsman cheese
Mozzarella balls

2—MEAT
N/A

3—PRODUCE
Blueberries
Dried apricots
Golden berries
Persian cucumbers

4—CRUNCH
Toasted crostini
Roasted almonds

5—DIP
Mixed berry jam

6—GARNISH
Fresh thyme
Mini roses

Bite Builder

- Huntsman + dried apricots + roasted almonds: *Sharp, sweet, and savory*
- Huntsman + mixed berry jam + toasted crostini: *Pungent, sweet, and crispy*
- Mozzarella + cucumbers + toasted crostini: *Creamy, fresh, and crunchy*
- Mozzarella + blueberries + mixed berry jam: *Fresh, juicy, and sweet*

1

3

4

5

6

that WOODSY WINTER *plate*

This plate is the most decadent cold-weather snack, perfect for a spread on a rustic tablescape. The baked fontina and gouda blend is topped with sweet fig jam and toasted almonds, accompanied by boiled potatoes, a fresh baguette, crispy radishes, and blanched asparagus. You also have my permission to go ahead and eat the gooey cheese with just a spoon. With fresh herbaceous notes of rosemary and basil, this plate captures a wide range of flavors to enjoy. Bake the cheese directly in the cast iron pan and serve immediately for ultimate gooeyness.

The Plate: CAST-IRON SKILLET, 8-INCH DIAMETER • SERVES 3 TO 4

1—CHEESE
Baked Fontina and Gouda with Fig Jam, Basil, and Slivered Almonds (recipe on page 214)

2—MEAT
N/A

3—PRODUCE
Red and pink radishes
Blanched asparagus
Boiled potatoes

4—CRUNCH
Baguette cubes

5—DIP
N/A

6—GARNISH
Fresh rosemary

Bite Builder

- Baked fontina and gouda + baguette cubes: ***Cheesy, sweet, and crisp***
- Baked fontina and gouda + potatoes: ***Gooey, nutty, and starchy***
- Baked fontina and gouda + radishes + asparagus: ***Decadent, garlicky, and crunchy***

- **TCP's favorite melting cheeses:** *Emmental, gruyère, raclette, fontina*

that OUTDOOR TERRACE *plate*

Summertime is my favorite time of year (as I was born on the summer solstice!). The sun sets later, the air is warm, and parties move outdoors. This plate features the sweet notes of summer—juicy stone fruit, creamy burrata, delicate sliced prosciutto, and fresh basil. Burrata, made by wrapping mozzarella around a luscious mixture of cream and cheese curds, is one of my favorite Italian cheeses. Take this plate out into the backyard, light some candles, and let the flavors play host. Check out page 16 for a flower arrangement to match.

The Plate: OVAL PORCELAIN PLATTER, 11 × 13 INCHES · SERVES 4 TO 5

1—CHEESE
Burrata

2—MEAT
Prosciutto

3—PRODUCE
Fresh apricots
Peaches
Persian cucumbers
Green grapes

4—CRUNCH
French baguette
Flatbread crackers
Pistachios

5—DIP
Extra-virgin olive oil

6—GARNISH
Fresh basil
Salt and pepper

Bite Builder

- Burrata + apricots + baguette: ***Creamy, juicy, and crispy***
- Burrata + prosciutto + cucumbers + flatbread crackers: ***Creamy, savory, fresh, and crunchy***
- Burrata + prosciutto + peaches: ***Silky, savory, and sweet***
- Burrata + grapes + pistachios + baguette: ***Decadent, juicy, salty, and crispy***

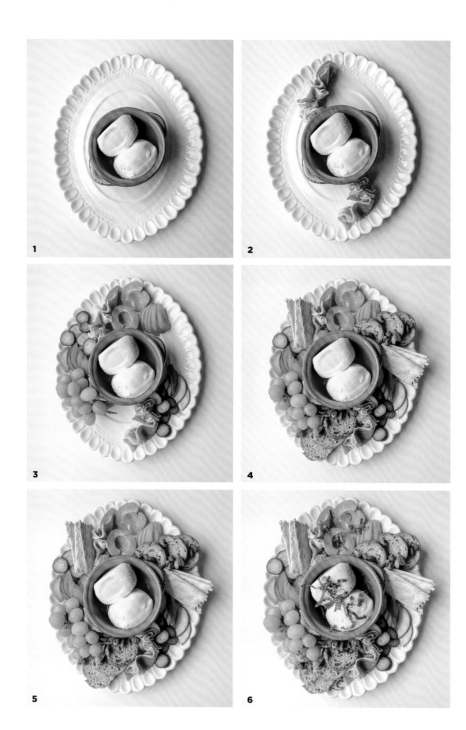

that SUMMER *in the* MOUNTAINS *plate*

Breathe in the beauty. Not much compares to the vast mountains in the summertime. Wildflowers peak out behind lush grass and a warm breeze saunters past. Perched up on a hilltop is a picnic table, set for lunch after a morning of exploring in nature. That's exactly where this cheese plate transports me. An herbes de Provence–infused toma cheese captures the herbaceous scents of the outdoors, while the whipped goat cheese with honey infuses the plate with a little sweetness.

The Plate: RECTANGULAR WOODEN BOARD, 9½ × 13½ INCHES · SERVES 3 TO 4

1—CHEESE
Toma Provence
Whipped goat cheese
with honey

2—MEAT
N/A

3—PRODUCE
Grapes
Blackberries
Blueberries
Dried apricots
Dried clementines

4—CRUNCH
Trail mix with chocolate
Fruit and nut crackers
Walnuts

5—DIP
Raspberry jam

6—GARNISH
Fresh rosemary
Edible violas

Bite Builder

- Toma Provence + dried apricots + fruit and nut crackers: ***Herby, sweet, and crunchy***
- Toma Provence + walnuts + raspberry jam: ***Nutty, crunchy, and fruity***
- Whipped goat cheese + blackberries + rosemary: ***Tangy, sweet, and herby***
- Whipped goat cheese + grapes + fruit and nut crackers: ***Creamy, juicy, and crunchy***

THAT CHEESE PLATE WANTS TO PARTY

that EVERYTHING SALSA *bowl*

This nod to salsa stems from my childhood. If you attend any Mullen barbecue or gathering in the summertime, this dish will be the star guest. I can remember the smell of fresh cilantro and lime in the kitchen, as my mom took her time chopping tomatoes, mango, onion, and avocado while draining corn and beans in the sink nearby. I also include cotija cheese—a Mexican semifirm cow's milk cheese that tastes like a buttery parmesan, adding a lovely level of saltiness to the dish. Mix together and serve alongside That Taco Tuesday Plate (page 194), or on its own with tortilla chips!

The Plate: **ROUND PORCELAIN BOWL, 9-INCH DIAMETER • SERVES 3 TO 4**

1—CHEESE
Cotija cheese

2—MEAT

N/A

3—PRODUCE
Red and orange grape tomatoes

Fresh mango
Cooked corn
Fresh jalapeños
Avocado
Red onion
Black beans

4—CRUNCH
Tortilla chips (on the side)

5—DIP
Lime juice

6—GARNISH
Fresh cilantro
Salt and pepper

that CRUNCHY GREENS *bowl*

Packed with healthy veggies and fresh goat cheese, this salad is the perfect summer staple to serve at your gatherings. Crunchy green apples, sugar snap peas, cucumbers, and watermelon radish are tossed over arugula with a miso dressing, which cuts through the slightly tangy and super creamy fresh chèvre. The salad is topped with pistachios and fresh herbs for a refreshing and light side dish.

The Plate: OVAL PORCELAIN PLATE, 15 × 10 INCHES • SERVES 4 TO 5

1—CHEESE
Chèvre

2—MEAT
N/A

3—PRODUCE
Sugar snap peas
Watermelon radishes
Persian cucumbers
Green apples
Arugula

4—CRUNCH
Pistachios

5—DIP
Miso dressing

6—GARNISH
Green onions
Fresh dill

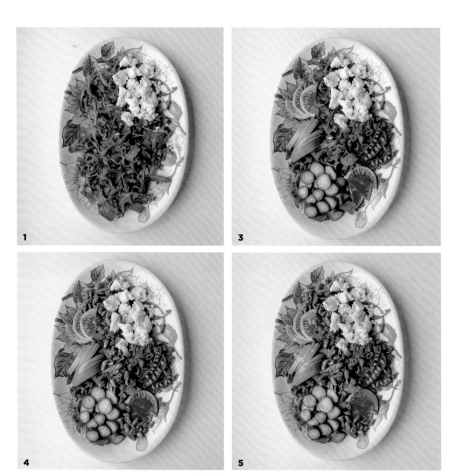

4

CHOOSE
A THEME

What better way to throw a party than crafting a plate themed to a specific holiday or celebration? This chapter is for the "out of the box" creations

and unconventional designs that let you have fun while impressing your guests. A cheese plate shaped like a wreath for the holidays? A heart-shaped creation for Valentine's Day? The opportunities are endless! To create these themed boards, I take my inspiration from the main elements for said event. For example, a bachelorette party celebrates a future marriage. So why not make the ring out of cheese? While the aesthetics behind these designs help set the party theme, I try to let the flavor pairings dictate these creations to ensure everything tastes just as good as it looks. With these plates, I'll guide you through stylistic techniques that get into the holiday spirit, while building on flavors that complement the theme.

A great way to set a theme on a plate is to use an unconventional garnish. This can be something like a themed cake topper, birthday candles, or even Christmas lights around the board. Just make sure you remove any nonedible garnishes before serving!

that GALENTINE'S *plate*

A soulmate is a term with many meanings. In short, it's a connection that feels comfortable, familiar, and at times, spiritual. A soulmate can be a romantic partner, a family member, or even a pet! Some of my deepest connections have been with my best girlfriends. Nothing beats sitting around a cheese plate, talking about the highs and lows of life itself. That is the true essence of Galentine's Day (or "Pal"-entines—it's not just for the ladies). This plate is loaded with some of my favorite cheeses and pairings, including a merlot-soaked cow's milk cheese, salami roses, and fresh honeycomb. Sweet, just like the friends who feel like family.

The Plate: HEART-SHAPED WOODEN BOARD, 12-INCH DIAMETER • SERVES 3 TO 4

1—CHEESE
Merlot BellaVitano
Camembert
Manchego

2—MEAT
Salami roses

3—PRODUCE
Dried cherries
Strawberries
Raspberries

4—CRUNCH
Biscuits
Sweet and Spicy Roasted
Walnuts (recipe on
page 233)
Prosecco chocolates

5—DIP
Fresh honeycomb

6—GARNISH
Fresh thyme

- **TCP's favorite camembert styles:** *Camembert Fermier, Hudson Valley Camembert, Green Hill*

that BACHELORETTE *plate*

Pack your bathing suits—we're headed to the beach! This plate is perfect for those tropical bachelorette parties, with a healthy yet decadent snack by the pool before hitting the town. Enjoy fresh mozzarella and basil and strawberry skewers, or dive into the goat brie diamond ring with a sweet strawberry champagne jam. I also added one of my favorite French cheeses, Comté—an alpine-style cow's milk cheese with a nutty base and slightly sweet finish. Full of fresh produce and bright colors, this plate will make the bride-to-be feel extra special.

The Plate: ROUND PORCELAIN PLATE, 14-INCH DIAMETER • SERVES 5 TO 6

1—CHEESE
Goat brie
Comté
Mozzarella skewers (mini mozzarella, strawberries, basil)

2—MEAT
Prosciutto

3—PRODUCE
Honeydew melon
Strawberries
Cantaloupe
Golden berries
Persian cucumbers

4—CRUNCH
Flatbread crackers

5—DIP
Strawberry champagne jam

6—GARNISH
Fresh mint
Fresh basil
Edible hibiscus flowers
Edible marigold petals

Bite Builder

- Goat brie + prosciutto + strawberry champagne jam: ***Creamy, salty, and sweet***
- Mozzarella skewer + cucumber + basil: ***Smooth, fresh, and fragrant***
- Mozzarella skewer + melon + mint: ***Fresh, sweet, and herbaceous***
- Comté + prosciutto + strawberry champagne jam: ***Nutty, savory, and sweet***

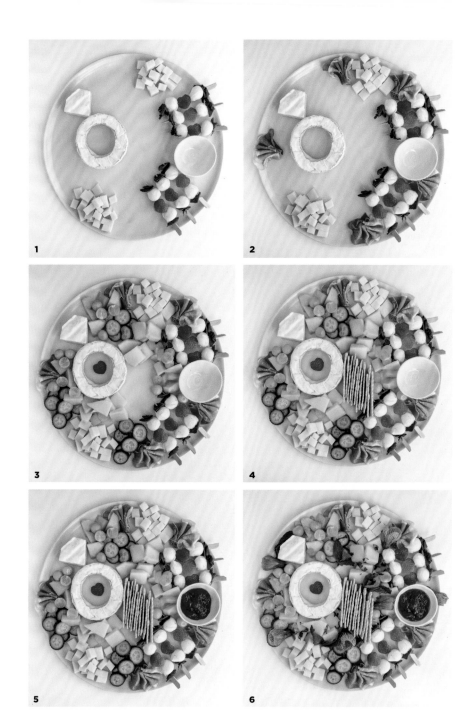

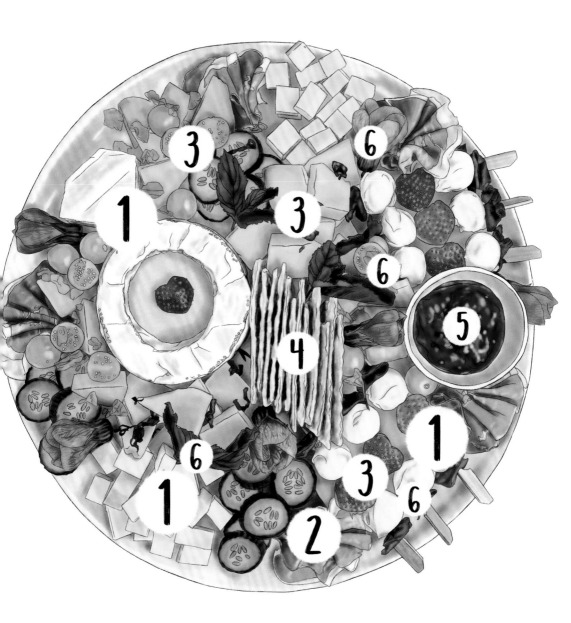

that BABY *on the* WAY *plate*

Serving snacks at baby showers can be tricky, as certain foods are best avoided while pregnant. I'm here to make it easy for you with this pregnancy-friendly cheese plate, designed to celebrate the mama-to-be and welcome the future kiddo! We skip the charcuterie on this board and feature hard, pasteurized cheese and a ton of nutritious fruits and vegetables. I like to "write" on the plate using letter-shaped vegetable cutters with purple radishes.

The Plate: ROUND CUT-OUT WOODEN BOARD, 14 × 11 INCHES • SERVES 5 TO 6

1—CHEESE
Ossau-Iraty
Aged gouda
Tête de Moine rosettes

2—MEAT
N/A

3—PRODUCE
Dried papaya
Blackberries
Blueberries
Purple radishes

4—CRUNCH
Honey sesame almonds
Cocoa-dusted cashews
Water crackers

5—DIP
Raspberry jam
Honeycomb

6—GARNISH
Fresh rosemary
Edible violas
Edible hibiscus flowers

Bite Builder

- Ossau-Iraty + raspberry jam + crackers: ***Creamy, sweet, and crunchy***
- Aged gouda + dried papaya + rosemary: ***Nutty, sweet, and fragrant***
- Aged gouda + cocoa-dusted cashews + raspberry jam: ***Smooth, chocolaty, and sweet***
- Tête de Moine + berries + honeycomb: ***Creamy, juicy, and sweet***

- **TCP's favorite tomme styles:** *Tomme de Savoie, Thomasville Tomme, Toma Piemontese*

that CHAR-BOO-TERIE *plate*

This is the ultimate spooky-season cheese and chocolate plate with a hint of childhood wonder. Picture this: You just got home from trick-or-treating and it's time to sort through your candy haul with your friends. Except now, it's an older, more refined Halloween party with unique cheeses to pair. Plus, the kids can still join in on the fun! On this plate we have four different cheeses—a lush French brie (in the shape of a ghost, naturally), a creamy cow's milk Port Salut, an ash-ripened goat cheese called Humboldt Fog, and aged cheddar. Try brie with a Kit Kat to resemble a creamy, chocolaty cake, or Humboldt Fog with chocolate-covered cherries to transform your bite with notes of cherry cheesecake. Don't let the combinations spook you! They're all delicious.

The Plate: RECTANGULAR WOODEN TRAY, 13 × 17 INCHES • SERVES 7 TO 8

1—CHEESE
French brie (cut with a ghost-shaped cookie cutter)
Humboldt Fog
Aged cheddar
Port Salut

2—MEAT
N/A

3—PRODUCE
Dried papaya
Dried figs
Dried apricots

4—CRUNCH
Dark-chocolate-covered cherries
Cocoa-dusted cashews
Chocolate-covered espresso beans
Salted Caramel and

Chocolate Popcorn Clusters (recipe on page 238)
Kit Kats
70% dark chocolate bars
Toasted hazelnuts

5—DIP
Apricot jam

6—GARNISH
Ant toothpicks

Bite Builder

- French brie + cocoa-dusted cashews + dried figs: ***Buttery, roasted, and fruity***
- Humboldt Fog + 70% dark chocolate + toasted hazelnuts: ***Tangy, sweet, and nutty***
- Aged cheddar + dried apricots + apricot jam: ***Sharp, sweet, and fruity***
- Port Salut + dried papaya + toasted hazelnuts: ***Creamy, sweet, and nutty***

that CHARCU-TURKEY plate

The charcu-turkey is charcuterie in the shape of a turkey, naturally. Thanksgiving is one of my favorite holidays at home. We take Thanksgiving food pretty seriously in the Mullen household, typically serving a traditional turkey, a smoked turkey, a ton of sides, and a plethora of pies. To gear up for the big meal, we need a festive cheese plate to set the mood. The charcu-turkey offers savory pairings to prep the palette, like smoked gouda and salame piccante, and more mild flavors for the less adventurous, like Colby Jack and dried figs. Building this board is also a fun activity to do with family—for the turkey's face, use two olives for the eyes, a radish nose, and a salami gobbler!

The Plate: ROUND CERAMIC PLATE, 15½-INCH DIAMETER • SERVES 4 TO 5

1—CHEESE
Smoked gouda
Mini mozzarella balls
Colby Jack
Sharp cheddar
Gruyère

2—MEAT
Salame piccante
Fennel salami

3—PRODUCE
Yellow bell pepper
Radishes
Cornichons
Kalamata olives
Persian cucumbers
Dried figs

4—CRUNCH
Truffle Marcona almonds
Pita crackers

5—DIP
N/A

6—GARNISH
Fresh rosemary

Bite Builder

- Smoked gouda + salame piccante + Marcona almonds: ***Robust, savory, and crunchy***
- Mozzarella + radishes + kalamata olives: ***Fresh, crunchy, and salty***
- Colby Jack + cornichons + fennel salami: ***Mild, sour, and savory***
- Gruyère + dried figs + pita crackers: ***Nutty, sweet, and crunchy***
- Sharp cheddar + yellow pepper + fennel salami: ***Sharp, fresh, crunchy, and savory***

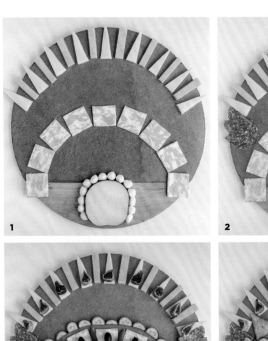

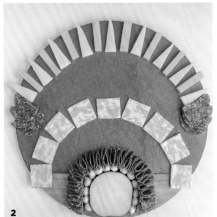

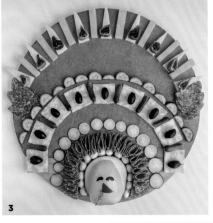

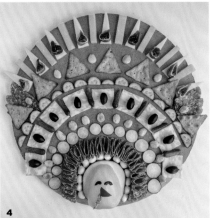

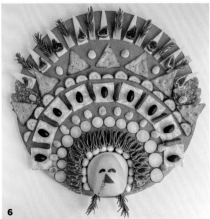

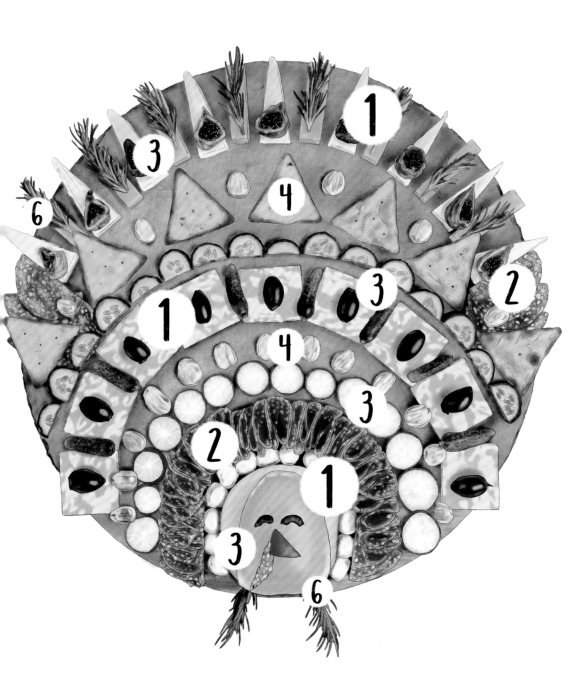

that LOADED LATKE *plate*

I grew up celebrating both Hanukkah and Christmas. Let's be honest, Christmas always tends to be the star. Now it's Hanukkah's time to shine. This plate takes potato latkes to the next level, homemade in a waffle maker and paired with lemon crème fraîche, charred scallions, and herbs. I even included caviar—we're getting fancy here! The havarti with dill ties into the herby dip, and smoked salmon adds some savory saltiness. For a kosher option, you can swap out the cheese with a plant-based cashew cheese. *L'chaim!*

The Plate: ROUND WOODEN PLATE, 15-INCH DIAMETER • SERVES 4 TO 5

1—CHEESE
Havarti with dill
Drunken Goat

2—MEAT
Smoked salmon
Chopped hard-boiled eggs
Caviar

3—PRODUCE
Watermelon radishes
Persian cucumbers
Pickled red onions

4—CRUNCH
Potato latke waffles
Flatbread crackers

5—DIP
Crème Fraîche with Lemon, Charred Scallions, Chives, and Dill (recipe on page 217)

6—GARNISH
Fresh dill

Bite Builder

- Dill havarti + smoked salmon + latke waffle: ***Herby, salty, creamy, and crispy***
- Dill havarti + pickled red onions + flatbread crackers: ***Creamy, sweet, sour, and crunchy***
- Drunken Goat + watermelon radishes + smoked salmon + latke waffle: ***Smooth, fresh, salty, and crispy***
- Caviar + hard-boiled egg + cucumbers + crème fraîche + latke waffle: ***Salty, savory, fresh, creamy, and crispy***
- Caviar + pickled red onions + crème fraîche + smoked salmon + latke waffle: ***Salty, briny, creamy, salty, and crispy***

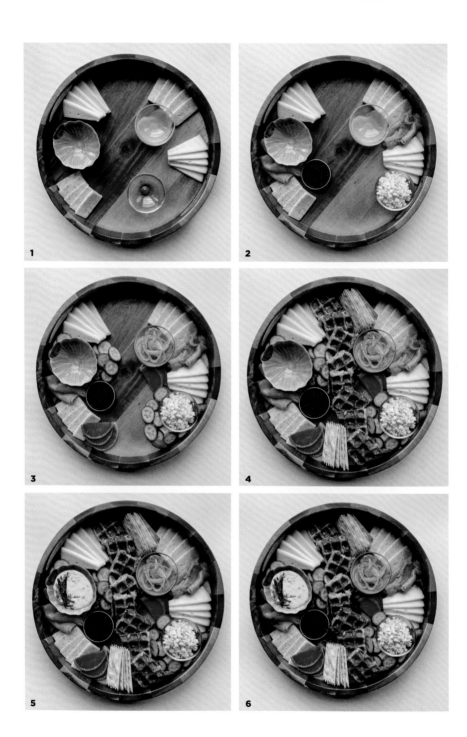

that CHARCUTER-WREATH *plate*

One cold winter day in 2019, I decided to make my very first "charcuter-wreath." It's exactly what you think it is: cheese and charcuterie styled in the shape of a wreath. Since then, this style has taken the Internet by storm, and the wreath is here to stay! I love its versatility—it sets a theme in a simple way, without the use of any crazy props or garnishes. Here, I drew inspiration from Italian antipasto notes—a nod to the food served at the Christmas parties I grew up attending. On this plate we have some classic pairings, like mozzarella, tomato, basil, and balsamic glaze, as well as a ton of freshly sliced charcuterie, such as mortadella, prosciutto di San Daniele, and spicy soppressata. I also made my own herby flatbread to serve alongside this plate.

The Plate: ROUND WOODEN LAZY SUSAN, 15-INCH DIAMETER • SERVES 5 TO 6

1—CHEESE
Pecorino Romano
Mini brie
Pearl mozzarella balls

2—MEAT
Prosciutto di San Daniele
Spicy soppressata
Mortadella

3—PRODUCE
Castelvetrano olives
Marinated mushrooms
Grape tomatoes

4—CRUNCH
Marcona almonds
Flatbread with Herbs and Gruyère (on the side; recipe on page 231)

5—DIP
Tomato chutney
Balsamic glaze

6—GARNISH
Fresh basil
Fresh rosemary

Bite Builder

- Pecorino Romano + prosciutto San Daniele + Marcona almonds + tomato chutney: ***Sharp, savory, and sweet***
- Pearl mozzarella balls + marinated mushrooms + mortadella + balsamic glaze: ***Smooth, tangy, savory, and sweet***
- Pearl mozzarella balls + grape tomatoes + balsamic glaze + basil: ***Creamy, juicy, sweet, and herbaceous***
- Mini brie + spicy soppressata + grape tomatoes + tomato chutney: ***Buttery, spicy, juicy, and sweet***

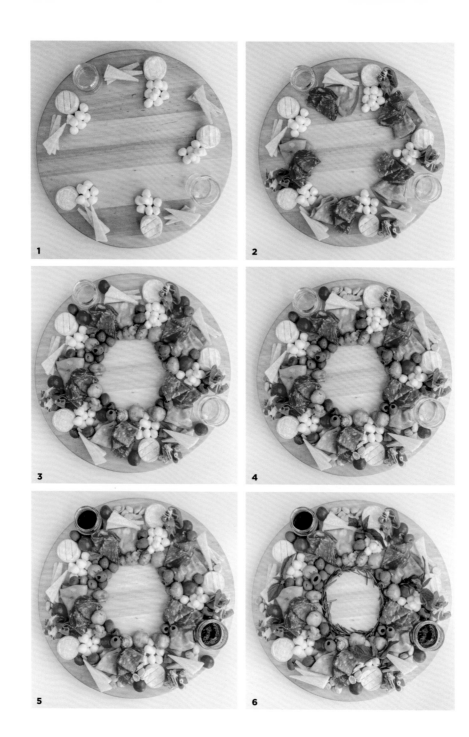

that FIND ME at MIDNIGHT plate

Time to upgrade your New Year's Eve party snacks. When I think of New Year's Eve, I'm reminded of decadent food, shimmering outfits, and gold accents. On this plate, we have a luscious and creamy Crémeux de Bourgogne (a French cow's milk cheese) paired with blackberries, Ferrero Rocher chocolates, and strawberry champagne jam. Who needs a midnight kiss when you can feel the euphoric rush of a delicious bite of cheese?! The perfect way to ring in the New Year, if you ask me. On this plate, we also have what I call the "napkin hack." Place a festive cocktail napkin in the center of your cheese plate and build around it. This is an easy way to set a theme without having to purchase too many crazy props!

The Plate: ROUND STONE PLATE, 18 INCHES • SERVES 7 TO 8

1—CHEESE
Queso Iberico
Crémeux de Bourgogne
Reserve cheddar
Beecher's Flagship
Harbison

2—MEAT
Italian dry salami

3—PRODUCE
Blackberries
Blueberries

4—CRUNCH
Ferrero Rocher chocolates
Dark chocolate with almonds
Mini stroopwafels
Prosecco chocolates

5—DIP
Fig and ginger jam
Strawberry champagne jam

6—GARNISH
Edible gold leaf
Dried rose petals

Bite Builder

- Queso Iberico + Italian dry salami + fig and ginger jam: **Grassy, savory, and sweet**
- Crémeux de Bourgogne + blackberries + dark chocolate with almonds: **Buttery, juicy, and sweet**
- Reserve cheddar + Italian dry salami + strawberry champagne jam: **Sharp, savory, and sweet**
- Beecher's Flagship + blueberries + stroopwafels: **Robust, juicy, and sweet**
- Harbison + blueberries + prosecco chocolates: **Buttery, juicy, and sweet**

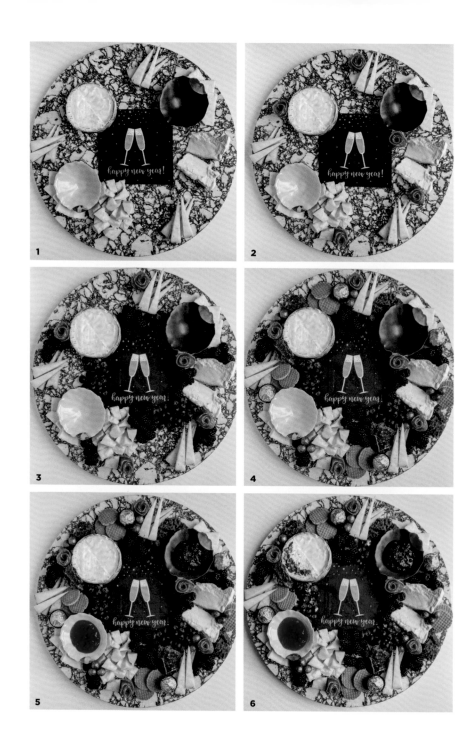

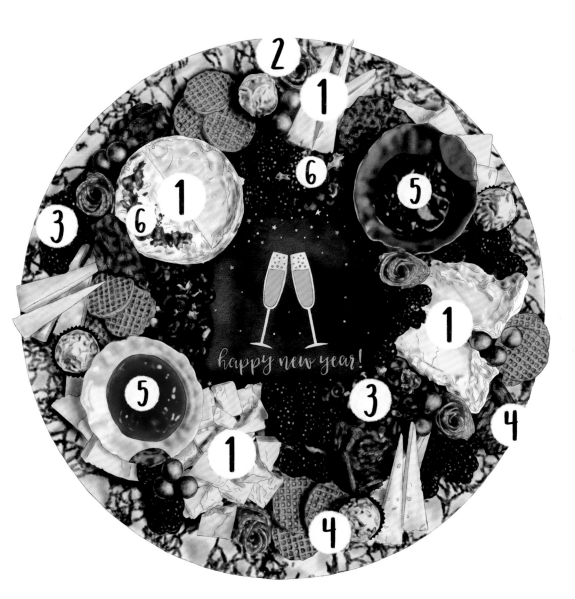

happy new year!

5

GATHER
TO GRAZE

While you can have an epic party no matter the size, location, or scenery, nothing beats a big spread to really take your celebration to the next level. Grazing tables might seem like an ambitious undertaking, but they're totally worth the final product.

Throughout this chapter, I show two different styles of grazes. First, we have an abundant and overflowing spread. Place butcher paper directly on the table, add your small plates and ramekins, and fill up the spaces on the butcher paper with cheese and accompaniments until the entire surface is plentiful. I also created another style which reflects a more simple and minimalist spread. For this technique, look around the house for a selection of trays, small plates, and bowls, and lay them out on the table to showcase your cheesy creations. Instead of putting food directly on butcher paper, use that blank space for garnishes, like flowers and greenery. This style almost looks like a still life, or a gallery wall of colorful food.

The creations in this chapter showcase how to build a grazing table in sections, so the process is easy to break down step by step using the Cheese By Numbers method. You can then multiply each section for the size gathering you're having. If you're having a large party, either prepare to refill the board, or make two or three plates of the same design side by side on the table. See page 17 for an example of a completed grazing table.

Grazing Table Tips

- If building directly on the table, use butcher paper to line the surface so you can fill up every blank space with food.
- Add your foundation, like platters, ramekins, flower vases, and candles, before setting down the cheese. You can also add cake stands for height, as well as baskets for additional crackers and bread.
- Prepping is key! Precut all hard cheeses, pre-fold meats, and slice produce and bread before starting to work on your grazing table, so the building process is easy and seamless.
- Take your time. Grazing tables are a big undertaking, but if you pace yourself and go step by step, it can be a meditative artistic activity!
- Aim to finish building the grazing table no earlier than thirty minutes before serving to guests to ensure freshness.

that CLASSIC GRAZE *plate*

This is your classic go-to grazing table for any occasion—colorful, tasteful, and easy to build with a wide variety of classic cheeses and delicious produce to pair. You can find the completed version of this grazing table on page 17, with suggested florals and a tablescape design. The cheeses here cover a wide range of flavor bases—buttery, pungent, herbaceous, nutty, and sharp. Paired with sweet and savory accompaniments, there's a perfect bite for everyone!

Foundation: BUTCHER PAPER (24 × 24 INCHES), 1 WOODEN PLATFORM (8-INCH DIAMETER), TWO 3-OUNCE RAMEKINS, TWO 4-OUNCE RAMEKINS, 1 BUD VASE WITH EUCALYPTUS • SERVES 11 TO 12

1—CHEESE
Brie
Point Reyes Bay Blue
Rosemary asiago
Aged gouda
Sharp cheddar

2—MEAT
Sliced Genoa salami
Hard salami

3—PRODUCE
Dried apricots
Concord grapes
Mandarin oranges
Persian cucumbers
Blueberries
Cornichons
Marinated olives

4—CRUNCH
French baguette
Flatbread crackers

Fruit and nut crackers
Pistachios
Unsalted mixed nuts

5—DIP
Local honey
Strawberry rhubarb jam

6—GARNISH
Edible flowers
Fresh rosemary
Fresh thyme

Bite Builder

- Brie + blueberries + honey + flatbread crackers: ***Creamy, juicy, sweet, and crunchy***
- Rosemary asiago + Genoa salami + cornichons: ***Sharp, salty, sour, and herbaceous***
- Aged gouda + hard salami + dried apricots + honey: ***Caramel, savory, jammy, and sweet***
- Sharp cheddar + Concord grapes + strawberry rhubarb jam + fruit and nut crackers: ***Robust, juicy, sweet, and crunchy***

- **TCP's favorite sharp cheddars:** *Prairie Breeze, Beecher's Flagship, Grafton Cheddar, Hook's 5-Year*

that BOUNTIFUL BIRTHDAY *plate*

They say you can't have your cake and eat it too . . . but if your cake is made of cheese, technically you can have both. This "cheese cake" is made from two incredible cheeses. The base is Harbison from Jasper Hill Farm, a soft-ripened cow's milk cheese wrapped in a spruce bark. It's buttery, woodsy, and sweet with vegetal flavors. On top of the Harbison is a blend of sheep's and cow's milk and the rind is washed with Graft cider. Happy early birthday to me (because, yes, I got to eat this after taking the photos). I also added some sharp cheddar, a Spanish sheep's milk cheese with edible flowers, cupcakes, macarons, cookies, and, of course, birthday candles!

Foundation (clockwise from top): ROUND MARBLE PLATE (9-INCH DIAMETER), RECTANGULAR WOODEN BOARD (7 × 8½ INCHES), ROUND PORCELAIN BOWL (5-INCH DIAMETER), 3-OUNCE RAMEKIN, OVAL PORCELAIN PLATE (7½ × 12 INCHES) • SERVES 10 TO 11

1—CHEESE
Queso de Oveja con Flores
Harbison (bloomy-rind
cow's milk cheese)
Washed rind sheep's and
cow's milk cheese
Reserve cheddar

2—MEAT
Sweet soppressata

3—PRODUCE
Strawberries
Raspberries
Blood oranges
Dried apricots

4—CRUNCH
Shortbread cookies
Macarons
Confetti cookies

Mini cupcakes
Mixed nuts

5—DIP
Honeycomb

6—GARNISH
"Happy birthday" cupcake
toppers
Dried edible flowers
Birthday candles

Bite Builder

- Queso de Oveja con Flores + sweet soppressata + dried apricots + honeycomb: **_Tangy, savory, and sweet_**
- Harbison + raspberries + shortbread cookies: **_Buttery, juicy, and sweet_**
- Washed rind sheep's and cow's milk cheese + strawberries + honeycomb: **_Creamy, juicy, and sweet_**
- Reserve cheddar + sweet soppressata + honeycomb: **_Robust, savory, and sweet_**

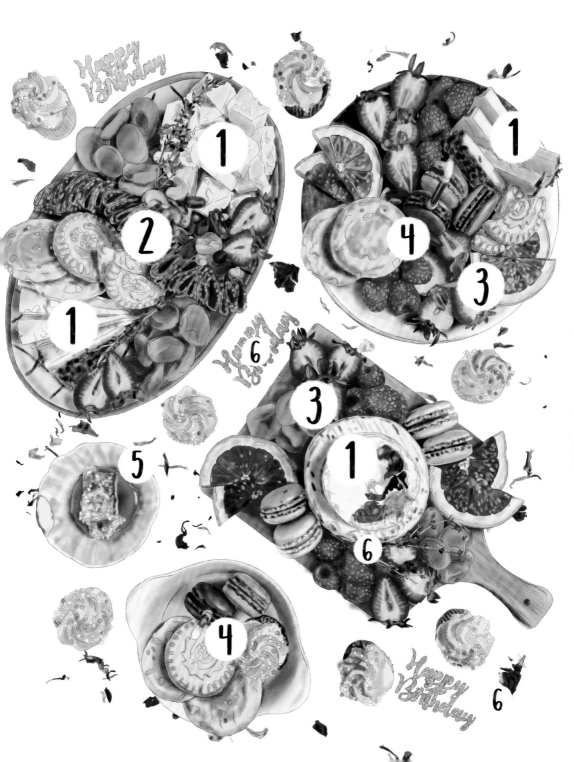

that HOT GRILL SUMMER *plate*

My dad and our family friends coined the term "appe-dog," and it's exactly what you think it is: an appetizer hot dog. It might sound completely unnecessary and indulgent, but the appe-dog is a staple at Mullen barbecues. Grilling reminds me of family gatherings, joyful celebrations, and the unofficial start of summer. Now that I live in Brooklyn and don't have any outdoor space, my grilling days are few and far between, so I venture out to the suburbs when I need a fix. This cheese plate is a perfect snacky meal or hefty appetizer to set up for any warm-weather gathering, from a beachy picnic to a Memorial Day barbecue. I also added in a summertime cheesy favorite: grilled halloumi. Halloumi is a goat's and cow's milk cheese from Cyprus. It has a high melting point, so it chars up perfectly for skewers on the barbecue.

Foundation (clockwise from top): OBLONG PORCELAIN PLATTER (5 × 6 INCHES), 3-OUNCE RAMEKIN, ROUND PORCELAIN PLATE (12-INCH DIAMETER), RECTANGULAR WOODEN BOARD (10 × 6 INCHES), OBLONG PORCELAIN PLATTER (5 × 6 INCHES), THREE 4-OUNCE RAMEKINS, WOODEN RECTANGULAR BOARD (7 × 8½ INCHES) • SERVES 4

1—CHEESE Grilled Pineapple, Pepper, and Halloumi Skewers (recipe on page 226)	Dill pickles Broccoli salad Sauerkraut	Yellow mustard Ketchup
2—MEAT Hot dogs	**4—CRUNCH** Pasta salad Wavy potato chips	**6—GARNISH** Fresh dill Yellow roses Rose leaves Blue thistles Fresh basil
3—PRODUCE Watermelon	**5—DIP** Sweet relish	

Ultimate Hot Dog

- Hot dog + relish + mustard + ketchup + sauerkraut + crumbled potato chips

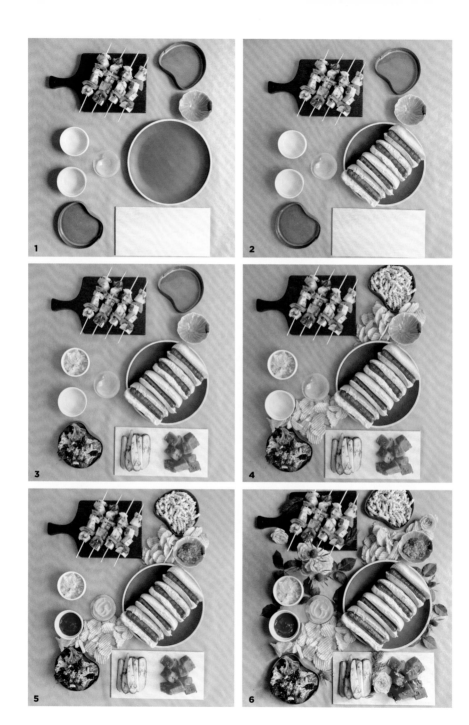

that TACO TUESDAY *plate*

I love the versatility of a taco. This spread obviously does not do authentic taco shops justice, but it's made with a combination of taco fixings that I love. I also included a delicious "everything salsa" that's bursting with flavor—something my mom used to make at every summer party growing up. This spread is easy to make—just set out a variety of plates and bowls, with cilantro, limes, and flowers to garnish.

Foundation: (clockwise from top): ROUND PORCELAIN BOWL WITH HANDLE (6½-INCH DIAMETER), TWO 4-OUNCE RAMEKINS, OVAL PORCELAIN PLATE (6 × 8½ INCHES), ROUND PORCELAIN BOWL WITH HANDLE (6-INCH DIAMETER), 3-OUNCE RAMEKIN, OVAL PORCELAIN PLATE (6 × 8½ INCHES), 1-OUNCE RAMEKIN • SERVES 5 TO 6

1—CHEESE
Cotija cheese
Shredded Mexican blend
(Monterey Jack, cheddar,
queso quesadilla, and asa-
dero cheeses)

2—MEAT
Marinated pulled pork
Spicy pulled chicken
Fajita-spiced jackfruit
(plant-based)

3—PRODUCE
Purple cabbage
Diced red onions
Diced jalapeños
Limes

4—CRUNCH
Tortillas (flour or corn)

5—DIP
Everything Salsa
(recipe on page 134)

Guacamole
Tomatillo salsa

6—GARNISH
Fresh cilantro
Marigolds
Eucalyptus
Carnations

Bite Builder

- Marinated pulled pork + Mexican cheese blend + red onions + guacamole + lime: ***Savory, sharp, zesty, and smooth***
- Spicy pulled chicken + cabbage + cotija cheese + tomatillo salsa + cilantro + lime: ***Juicy, crunchy, creamy, herbaceous, and zesty***
- Spicy pulled chicken + Everything Salsa + cabbage + lime: ***Spicy, sweet, crunchy, and zesty***
- Fajita-spiced jackfruit + cotija cheese + jalapeños + cabbage + guacamole + lime: ***Robust, salty, spicy, crunchy, and smooth***

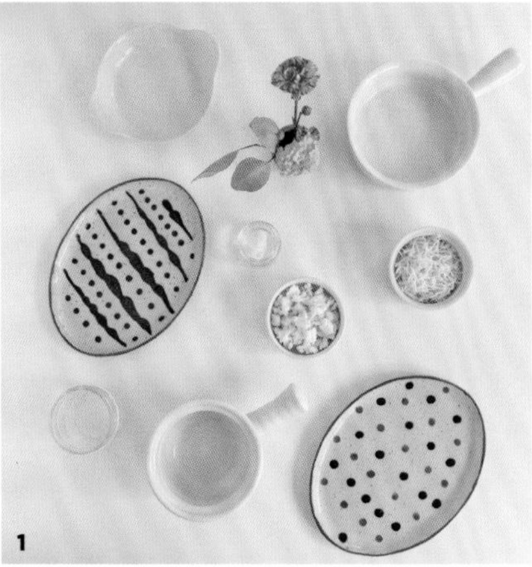
1

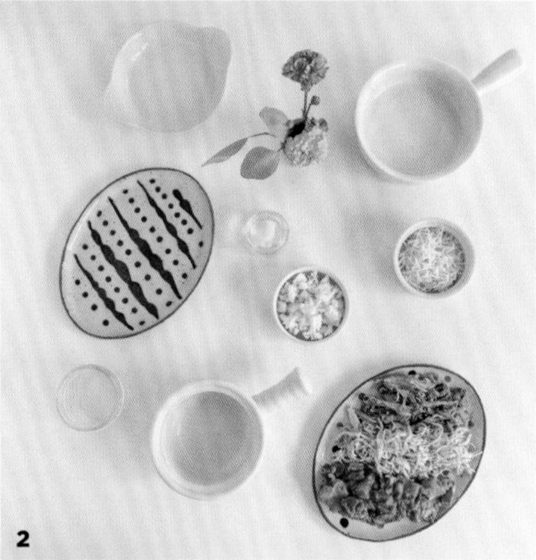
2

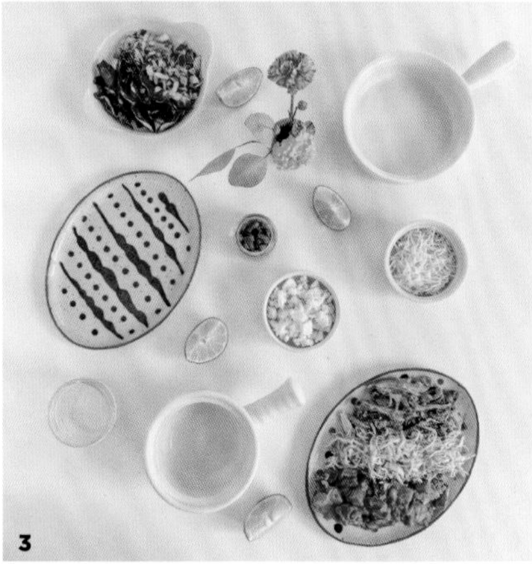
3

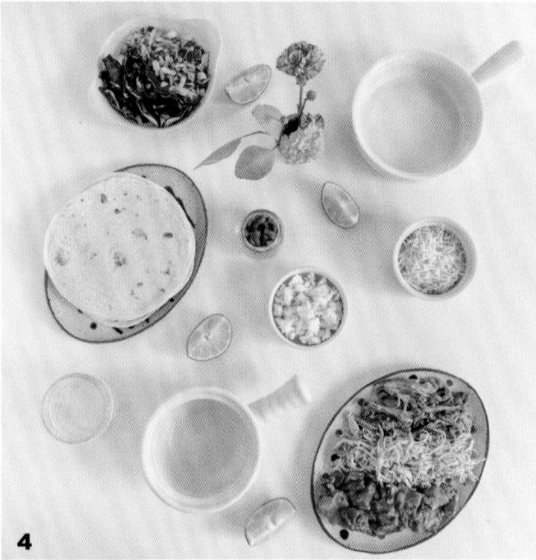
4

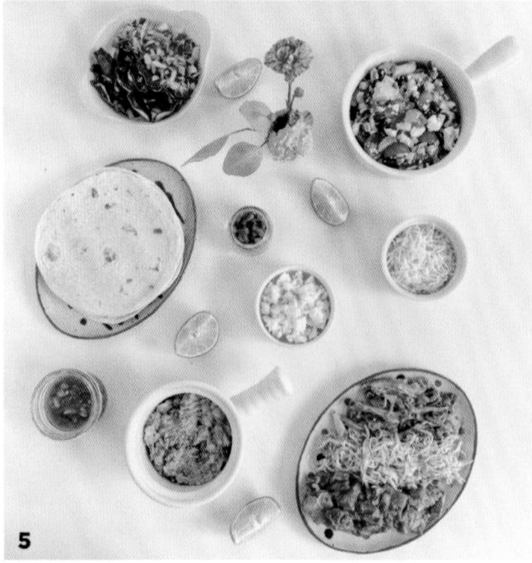
5

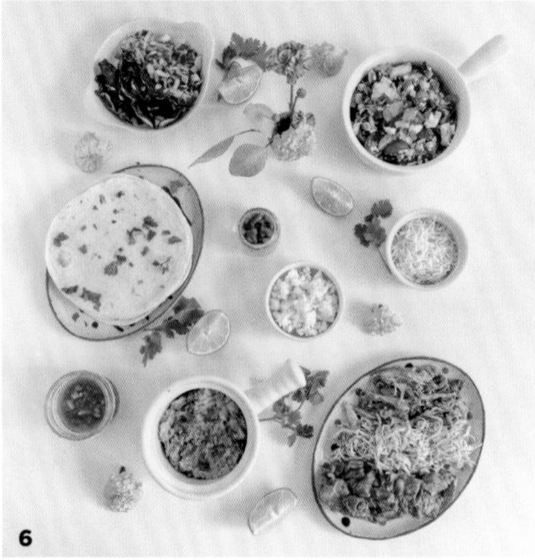
6

that TOUCHDOWN *plate*

It's game day! This grazing table has it all: a warm buffalo artichoke dip, crispy popcorn chicken, gooey mozzarella sticks, sharp cheddar, and a smoked bacon gouda. I had to balance out the gluttony with some colorful fresh cucumbers, celery, peppers, and carrots. This graze is best served hot, so I recommend prepping produce and folding your meat ahead of time so assembly is quick and easy. A fun way to dress up your dip is by turning it into a football—I used raw red peppers for the laces, which ties the creation together. Go Team Cheese Plate!

Foundation: BUTCHER PAPER (22 × 22 INCHES), 6-OUNCE BOWL, 3-OUNCE RAMEKIN, 8-OUNCE BOWL, 4-OUNCE BOWL, OVAL PORCELAIN BOWL (4½ × 8 INCHES) • SERVES 8 TO 10

1—CHEESE
Cheesy Buffalo Artichoke Dip (recipe on page 218)
Sharp cheddar
Smoked bacon gouda

2—MEAT
Spicy soppressata
Genoa salami
Popcorn chicken

3—PRODUCE
Red peppers
Cucumbers
Celery
Yellow peppers
Rainbow carrots

4—CRUNCH
Pretzel chips
Wavy potato chips
Dijon spiced pistachios
Mozzarella sticks

5—DIP
Buffalo sauce
Ranch dressing

6—GARNISH
Cilantro

Bite Builder

- Cheesy Buffalo Artichoke Dip + potato chips + celery: ***Creamy, crunchy, and fresh***
- Sharp cheddar + spicy soppressata + cucumber: ***Sharp, spicy, and fresh***
- Sharp cheddar + Genoa salami + red pepper: ***Robust, savory, and sweet***
- Smoked bacon gouda + Genoa salami + pretzel chips: ***Savory, salty, and crunchy***
- Popcorn chicken + buffalo sauce + ranch: ***Savory, spicy, and creamy***

that SANDWICH SAMPLER *plate*

This sandwich spread is telling you two things: (1) Yes, you can make a sandwich on cheesy garlic bread; nobody is stopping you. (2) Let's embrace presliced cheese. If you want to take it up a notch, try making a turkey and brie sandwich with the luscious, buttery, triple crème brie, or a robust ham and cheese sandwich with a few slices of sharp and nutty Beecher's Flagship. That Sandwich Sampler Plate has no rules. Encourage your guests to get creative with it!

Foundation (clockwise from top): **WOODEN RECTANGULAR BOARD (11 × 15 INCHES), THREE 3-OUNCE RAMEKINS, PORCELAIN BOWL (5 INCHES), WOODEN RECTANGULAR BOARD (9½ × 13½ INCHES), WOODEN RECTANGULAR BOARD (10 × 6 INCHES), WOODEN SQUARE BOARD (8 × 8 INCHES), WOODEN RECTANGULAR BOARD (9½ × 13½ INCHES)** • SERVES 4 TO 5

1—CHEESE
Sharp cheddar
Colby Jack
Beecher's Flagship
Monterey Jack
Pepper Jack
Triple crème brie

2—MEAT
Black Forest ham
Turkey
Mortadella

3—PRODUCE
Mesclun mix
Bread and butter pickles
Red onions
Persian cucumbers
Tomatoes

4—CRUNCH
Dill pickle potato chips
Cheesy Basil Garlic Bread
(recipe on page 234)
Mini French rolls

5—DIP
Dijon mustard
Whole-grain mustard
Mayonnaise

6—GARNISH
Fresh basil
Ranunculus flowers
(for the table)

Sandwich Builder

- Triple crème brie + turkey + mesclun + cucumbers + Dijon mustard
- Sharp cheddar + turkey + mesclun + cucumbers + basil + Dijon mustard + mayo
- Pepper Jack + turkey + mesclun + tomato + dill pickle potato chips + mayo
- Beecher's Flagship + Black Forest ham + bread and butter pickles + whole-grain mustard
- Monterey Jack + mortadella + red onions + bread and butter pickles + mayo + Dijon mustard
- Cheesy Basil Garlic Bread + cucumbers + tomatoes + red onions + basil

that TAPAS BAR *plate*

Spanish tapas are one of my favorite ways to snack. I can't help but order way too many small plates, but then I relish all the delicious flavors. On this plate, I have three different types of Manchego—a three-month, six-month, and eight-month. Younger Manchego tends to have aromas of sweet, tangy flavors, like sour cream and cheesecake. As the cheese ages, it develops more of a rounded, nutty flavor, with intense and zesty notes. I also added some classic tapas dishes like patatas bravas (spicy potatoes) and pan con tomate (bread with tomato).

Foundation (clockwise from top): **RECTANGULAR WOODEN BOARD (7 × 8½ INCHES), ROUND WOODEN BOARD (9-INCH DIAMETER), 3-OUNCE GLASS RAMEKIN, OVAL PORCELAIN BOWL (4½ × 8 INCHES), 6-OUNCE CERAMIC BOWL, TWO HALF-MOON PLATES (4 × 9 INCHES), 4-OUNCE BOWL, SMALL PORCELAIN PLATE (5-INCH DIAMETER)** • **SERVES 8 TO 10**

1—CHEESE
Manchego 3-month
Manchego 6-month
Manchego 8-month

2—MEAT
Sardines
Iberico chorizo
Serrano ham

3—PRODUCE
Pepperoncini

Assorted marinated olives
Green olives
Pimento peppers
Dates
Tomato on the vine

4—CRUNCH
Baguette
Pan con tomate
Patatas bravas

5—DIP
Extra-virgin olive oil
Fig, Sweet Onion,
and Rosemary Jam
(recipe on page 241)

6—GARNISH
Fresh rosemary
Fresh thyme
Carnations
Greenery

Bite Builder

- Manchego 3-month + serrano ham + Fig, Sweet Onion, and Rosemary Jam: ***Tangy, salty, and sweet***
- Manchego 6-month + Iberico chorizo + green olives: ***Robust, savory, and salty***
- Manchego 8-month + dates + Fig, Sweet Onion, and Rosemary Jam: ***Nutty, sweet, and herbaceous***
- Sardines + pepperoncini + pan con tomate + olive oil: ***Salty, briny, and crunchy***

recipes

Like making a cheese plate, cooking is magic. By combining a few simple items, you create a new dish that's bursting with flavor and character. I love to elevate my cheese plates with unique recipes that push these elements to a new level. Dates are delicious on a cheese plate just by themselves, but something amazing happens when you stuff them with blue cheese and candied ginger. These dishes can be served on your plate itself, or alongside as part of the tablescape spread. Mix and match dishes and cheese plates for the ultimate party food experience!

everything bagel seasoned whipped feta

This recipe makes for an excellent party dip and bagel shmear alike. With a smooth blend of creamy feta and Greek yogurt, the briny, tangy, and salty flavors merge wonderfully. I will also never get tired of everything bagel seasoning. I still put it on everything.

makes 1½ cups • time: 15 minutes

1 (8-ounce) block Greek feta

4 ounces (½ cup) plain 2% Greek yogurt

3 tablespoons extra-virgin olive oil, plus more for drizzling

1½ tablespoons lemon juice (from about half a large lemon)

1 tablespoon chopped fresh dill fronds, plus more for garnish

1 tablespoon chopped fresh parsley leaves, plus more for garnish

1 tablespoon everything bagel seasoning, plus more for garnish

Sliced scallion, for garnish

1. In a food processor, blend the feta, Greek yogurt, 3 tablespoons olive oil, and lemon juice until smooth. If needed, add more olive oil for a smoother consistency.
2. Add the dill, parsley, and everything bagel seasoning. Pulse to combine.
3. Spoon into a serving bowl and top with more everything bagel seasoning, dill, parsley, scallion, and a drizzle of olive oil.
4. The whipped feta will keep in the refrigerator in an airtight container for up to 3 days.

213

RECIPES

baked fontina and gouda with fig jam, basil, and slivered almonds

This dip is the ultimate party hit. Inspired by Ina Garten's baked fontina, we take it up a notch with gouda, fig jam, basil, and toasted almonds. Like gruyère, raclette, and Emmental, fontina and young gouda are excellent melting cheeses. Their mild flavor acts as a great base to build upon, and you can dress up melted cheese with everything from spicy honey to crisped prosciutto and roasted red peppers. The possibilities are endless. Serve this one straight out of the oven with crusty bread, boiled potatoes, and vegetables, as seen on page 123.

serves 4 • time: 15 minutes

2 ounces slivered almonds

8 ounces fontina, cut into 1-inch cubes

6 ounces young gouda, cut into 1-inch cubes

2 tablespoons extra-virgin olive oil

2 garlic cloves, minced

1 tablespoon chopped fresh basil leaves, plus more for garnish

¼ cup fig jam

1 baguette, or other loaf of crusty bread, for serving

1. Preheat the oven to 350°F. Place the almonds on a sheet pan and bake for about 6 minutes, until toasted. Remove from the oven.

2. Place a rack in the upper third of the oven (about 5 inches from the heat source) and heat the broiler to high.

3. Place the fontina and gouda in an 8-inch cast-iron skillet. Top with the olive oil, garlic, and basil. Broil for 5 minutes, until the cheese is bubbling and slightly browned.

4. Remove the cheese from the oven and top with the almonds, fig jam, and additional basil to garnish. Serve immediately with crusty bread.

crème fraîche with lemon, charred scallions, chives, and dill

Crème fraîche is like sour cream, but a bit thicker, less tangy, and deliciously creamy. This simple base makes for the perfect mild flavor to build upon. For this dip, we char some scallions over high heat, add a zing of lemon and lemon zest, and freshen it up with herbaceous dill and chives. This dip is a great pairing for your super salty and savory snacks, like smoked salmon or caviar. It also goes great on a potato latke!

makes 1½ cups • time: 20 minutes

1 tablespoon extra-virgin olive oil, plus more as needed

1 garlic clove, minced

1 small shallot, diced small

Kosher salt and freshly ground black pepper

5 scallions, 4 left whole, 1 with green portion thinly sliced

8 ounces (1 cup) crème fraîche or sour cream

4 ounces (½ cup) cream cheese, softened

2 tablespoons chopped fresh chives, plus more for garnish

2 tablespoons chopped fresh dill, plus more for garnish

2 teaspoons lemon juice

½ teaspoon onion powder

¼ teaspoon grated lemon zest

1. In a small frying pan, heat 1 tablespoon of the oil over medium-high heat. Add the garlic and shallot and sauté, stirring often, until lightly browned and fragrant, about 5 minutes. Season with salt and pepper and transfer directly to the food processor. Wipe out the skillet, drizzle the pan with a splash of oil, and add the 4 unsliced scallions. Cook over high heat, tossing every minute until charred, about 4 minutes. Season with salt and pepper.

2. In a food processor, combine the crème fraiche, charred scallions, cream cheese, chives, dill, lemon juice, onion powder, and a drizzle of olive oil with the sautéed garlic and shallots. Blend until smooth.

3. Add salt and pepper to taste. Puree in additional olive oil by the teaspoon if the dip is difficult to blend.

4. Spoon the dip into a bowl and top with additional dill and chives, the reserved sliced fresh scallion, lemon zest, and a drizzle of olive oil.

5. Serve immediately or refrigerate in an airtight container for up to 2 days.

cheesy buffalo artichoke dip

This dip is similar to a creamy spinach artichoke dip (but ditch the spinach, and add buffalo sauce). I used Greek yogurt and feta as my base, creating a savory, tangy flavor profile that contrasts wonderfully against the briny artichokes and spicy buffalo sauce. To make things extra cheesy, I mixed in and topped the dip with a four-cheese blend of fontina, parmesan, asiago, and mozzarella. Perfect for game day or whenever you crave a warm and decadent dish.

makes 1½ cups • time: 25 minutes

4 ounces Greek feta

2 ounces (¼ cup) Greek yogurt

4 marinated artichokes, drained

¼ cup shredded 4-cheese blend,
    plus more for garnish

About 1½ tablespoons Frank's RedHot
    Buffalo Wings Sauce

2 scallions, roughly chopped

1 tablespoon chopped fresh chives,
    plus more for garnish

2 tablespoons extra-virgin olive oil

1½ teaspoons lemon juice

¼ teaspoon garlic powder

¼ teaspoon onion powder

Kosher salt and freshly ground
    black pepper

1. Preheat the oven to 400°F.

2. In a food processor, puree the feta, Greek yogurt, artichokes, shredded cheese, ½ tablespoon of the buffalo sauce, 1 scallion, the chives, olive oil, lemon juice, garlic powder, and onion powder until smooth. Season with salt and pepper to taste. If you want the dip spicier, blend in an additional ½ tablespoon buffalo sauce.

3. Spoon into a 5 × 7-inch baking dish and top with additional shredded cheese and a drizzle of buffalo sauce.

4. Bake for 17 to 20 minutes, until the cheese topping has melted and the dip is bubbling. Top with the remaining scallion pieces and serve immediately.

one-pan baked goat cheese with chickpeas and broccoli

This simple one-dish meal features baked fresh goat cheese, chickpeas, broccoli, briny olives, and spicy Peppadews. This can be eaten on its own, spooned into a warm pita, or served as a dip with crusty bread. You could even use it to top cooked pasta. The combination of the tangy, creamy goat cheese and generous amounts of garlic and herbs makes for the best-tasting (and smelling) dish to enjoy any night you want to have a cheese party.

serves 2 to 3 • time: 45 minutes

8 ounces fresh goat cheese, at
    room temperature

4 ounces assorted pitted olives
    (such as Castelvetrano, kalamata,
    Niçoise, Ligurian)

4 ounces Peppadew peppers

1 (15.5-ounce) can chickpeas, rinsed
    and drained

4 ounces broccoli (about half a medium
    head), sliced into 2-inch florets

3 garlic cloves, chopped

½ teaspoon onion powder

¼ teaspoon red pepper flakes

¼ teaspoon kosher salt

¼ teaspoon freshly ground black pepper

¼ cup extra-virgin olive oil

1 tablespoon lemon juice

1 teaspoon fresh thyme leaves, chopped

1 teaspoon fresh rosemary leaves,
    chopped

Pita, sliced baguette, or other type of
    bread, or cooked pasta, for serving

1. Preheat the oven to 400°F.
2. Place the goat cheese in the center of an 8 × 10-inch baking dish. Scatter the olives, Peppadews, chickpeas, and broccoli around the cheese.
3. Sprinkle the garlic, onion powder, red pepper flakes, salt, and black pepper over the cheese and vegetables, then drizzle the olive oil over the top.
4. Bake for 30 to 40 minutes, until the broccoli is cooked through and the chickpeas are crisp.
5. Sprinkle the lemon juice and fresh herbs over the top. Serve immediately with bread or pasta.

herby purple potato salad

As I write this recipe, I'm witnessing the first signs of spring in New York. The temperature has finally reached 60 degrees, tree buds are forming, and the first little green daffodil leaves are making their way out of the garden beds. Springtime is when the world comes alive again, and this coincides with zesty fresh flavors to make our palates come alive! This purple potato salad isn't just beautiful, it also has tangy and sweet notes with bright herbs. This dish is perfect for your springtime plates and gatherings to serve alongside your cheese plate creations.

serves 3 to 4 • prep time: 10 minutes • marinating time: 2 to 4 hours

1 pound 2-inch purple potatoes, scrubbed

Kosher salt

2 tablespoons lemon juice (from about ⅔ of a large lemon)

1 tablespoon Dijon mustard

½ teaspoon red wine vinegar

1½ teaspoons honey

¼ cup extra-virgin olive oil

½ small red onion, halved crosswise and thinly sliced into half-moons

1½ tablespoons chopped fresh dill fronds, plus more for garnish

1½ teaspoons chopped fresh chives, plus more for garnish

2 scallions, thinly sliced, reserving some for garnish

Flaky salt and freshly ground black pepper

1. Cut the potatoes into quarters. Place in a medium saucepan and cover with water. Generously salt the water and bring to a boil, then reduce the heat and simmer for 4 to 5 minutes, until the potatoes can be easily pierced with a fork. Drain and place in a medium bowl.

2. In a small bowl, combine the lemon juice, mustard, vinegar, honey, olive oil, and 1 teaspoon kosher salt. Whisk until fully emulsified. Add the red onion, reserving some for garnish, and mix in the dill, chives, and scallions.

3. Pour the herb mixture over the potatoes and mix. Add flaky salt and black pepper to taste.

4. For the best flavor, marinate in the refrigerator for 2 to 4 hours. Garnish with the additional dill, chives, scallions, and the reserved red onion before serving. The potato salad will last for up to 2 days in the refrigerator.

seared crispy mushrooms with grana padano

I would argue that mushrooms may be one of the world's most versatile vegetables (after potatoes, of course). Mushrooms can be sautéed, grilled, steamed, and even fried into a plant-based meat alternative. This recipe takes mushrooms to the ultimate level of cheesy crispiness. You can use whatever variety of shroomies you'd like—the key is a hot skillet and patience. At the end we add shredded Grana Padano, a sharp and robust cow's milk cheese from Northern Italy, for a salty and flavorful kick. The result will transport you to a different state of mind.

serves 2 to 3 • time: 25 minutes

3 tablespoons extra-virgin olive oil

12 ounces mixed mushrooms (such as shiitake and cremini), sliced ¼ inch thick

Kosher salt and freshly ground black pepper

2 garlic cloves, minced

4 sprigs fresh thyme, leaves stripped from stems

3 tablespoons freshly grated Grana Padano

1. Heat 2 tablespoons of the olive oil in a 12-inch skillet over medium-high heat until hot.

2. Add half of the mushrooms in a single layer and cook, undisturbed, for about 5 minutes, until golden brown. Flip and let cook, undisturbed, on the other side for about 3 minutes. Remove and place on a small plate. Season with salt and pepper.

3. Add an additional tablespoon of olive oil to the pan and repeat with the remaining mushrooms. Once browned, return all the mushrooms to the pan and mix.

4. Reduce the heat to medium and add the garlic and thyme leaves. Cook, stirring, until the garlic is fragrant, about 1 minute.

5. Sprinkle the cheese directly over the mushrooms in the skillet, then serve immediately.

grilled pineapple, pepper, and halloumi skewers

Halloumi is a semisoft cheese from Cyprus, typically made with goat's and sheep's milk. The unique texture can be described as "squeaky," but it makes for an excellent grilling cheese. It has a salty, creamy, and complex flavor that complements sweet and vegetal notes. In this recipe, we pair halloumi with sweet pineapple and peppers in skewer form, perfect for your summertime BBQ parties.

makes 8 to 10 skewers • time: 10 minutes

1 pound halloumi, patted dry and cut into 1-inch cubes

2½ cups fresh pineapple, cut into 1-inch cubes

2 large sweet bell peppers, cut into 1-inch pieces

2 tablespoons extra-virgin olive oil

Honey, for drizzling

1 tablespoon lemon juice (about half a medium lemon)

2 tablespoons chopped fresh dill

Red pepper flakes (optional)

Kosher salt and freshly ground black pepper

1. If using wood or bamboo skewers, soak 8 to 10 of them in water for 30 minutes before using to avoid catching fire. Thread the halloumi, pineapple, and peppers onto the skewers. Transfer to a sheet pan and brush the loaded skewers with olive oil on all sides.

2. Heat a grill to medium-high, about 400°F. If using a charcoal grill, arrange the coals on one side of the grill for indirect heating. Let the grates heat for at least 10 minutes before grilling. (Alternatively, heat a grill pan on the stove over medium-high—no need to soak the skewers if cooking this way.) Grill the skewers for about 4 minutes, rotating them until the cheese is browned and the pineapple and peppers have a good char.

3. Remove from heat and transfer the skewers to a serving dish. Garnish with a drizzle of honey, the lemon juice, dill, and red pepper flakes for some heat, if desired. Season with salt and pepper and serve immediately.

buffalo mozzarella caprese

Nothing beats the pure luxurious decadence of buffalo mozzarella. Hailing from the region of Campania, Italy, this cheese is made from fresh buffalo milk. This creates a mozzarella that is creamier, softer, and much more flavorful than cow's milk mozzarella. Anytime I see a caprese salad at a party, I dive in headfirst. This recipe is a riff on a classic caprese, with an addition of Castelvetrano olives for some extra brininess and fresh cucumbers for a crunch. If you can't find buffalo mozzarella at your local grocery store, cow's milk mozz will do.

serves 2 to 4 · time: 10 minutes

5 ounces buffalo mozzarella, cut into
    1-inch bite-size pieces

6 ounces (1 cup) yellow grape tomatoes,
    halved

2 Persian cucumbers, halved lengthwise
    and sliced

2½ ounces (½ cup) pitted Castelvetrano
    olives, roughly chopped

1 tablespoon chopped fresh basil leaves

2 tablespoons extra-virgin olive oil

1 tablespoon lemon juice

2 teaspoons balsamic vinegar

Kosher salt and freshly ground
    black pepper

1. In a medium bowl, combine the mozzarella, tomatoes, cucumbers, olives, and basil. Toss with the olive oil, lemon juice, and balsamic vinegar. Season with salt and pepper to taste. Serve immediately or store in the refrigerator for up to 2 days.

flatbread with herbs and gruyère

AS SEEN ON THAT CHARCUTER-WREATH PLATE

Stovetop flatbread is a simple way to make that "crunch" stand out for your cheese plate creations. With a few simple ingredients, these fluffy and flavorful flatbreads can be served alongside soft and hard cheeses alike. They're also extremely customizable. Add in herbs, cheese, and spices for an extra notch of flavor. This is my go-to recipe when I want a no-bake bread option for my gatherings!

makes 8 flatbreads • time: 55 minutes

1¼ cups lukewarm water

1 (¼-ounce) packet (2 teaspoons)
    instant yeast

1 pinch of granulated sugar

3 cups (375 grams) all-purpose flour,
    plus more for rolling the dough

3 tablespoons olive oil, plus more
    for the pan

1 teaspoon kosher salt

1 cup shredded gruyère

2 tablespoons chopped fresh parsley

2 tablespoons chopped fresh basil

1. Mix the water, yeast, and sugar in a medium mixing bowl with a fork until the yeast dissolves. Let sit for 5 to 10 minutes, until foamy.

2. Add the flour, 2 tablespoons of the oil, and salt and mix until a cohesive, shaggy dough forms.

3. Scrape the dough onto a well-floured surface and knead with floured hands for 10 minutes, until smooth. The dough will be sticky, so reflour your hands or use a bench scraper if needed. Coat the bottom of the bowl with the remaining tablespoon of oil, and place the dough back in the bowl, turning to coat with the oil. Cover loosely with a dish towel and let sit in a warm spot for 30 to 45 minutes, until doubled in size.

4. After the dough rises, turn it out onto a floured surface and cut into 8 even pieces. Roll each piece of dough into a 6-inch round and sprinkle each with equal amounts of cheese and herbs, leaving a 1-inch border. Fold the edges of the dough into the center and reroll into a 6-inch round. Pop any air bubbles.

5. Coat a large cast-iron pan with a thin layer of oil and heat over medium heat until the oil ripples. Place one flatbread in the skillet and cook for about 2 minutes, until golden brown and puffed up like a pita, then flip and cook for another 2 minutes. Re-oil the pan and repeat with the remaining flatbreads. To keep the breads warm, place on a sheet pan in a 200°F oven, or wrap in a kitchen towel. Serve warm.

sweet and spicy roasted walnuts

AS SEEN ON THAT GALENTINE'S PLATE

Let's take a normal walnut and elevate it to the next level. These sweet and spicy roasted walnuts are a great addition to a cheese plate, acting as a crunchy and savory partner for nutty and sharp cheeses like Manchego and cheddar. This recipe also works for other nuts, such as cashews, pecans, and almonds.

makes 2 cups • time: 50 minutes

1 egg white

1 tablespoon maple syrup

1 teaspoon chili powder

⅛ teaspoon cayenne pepper

½ teaspoon salt

2 cups raw, unsalted walnuts

1. Preheat the oven to 300°F and line a sheet pan with parchment paper.
2. In a medium bowl, whisk the egg white and 1½ teaspoons water until frothy with bubbles.
3. Add the maple syrup, chili powder, cayenne, and salt; stir to combine. Add the nuts and toss to fully coat with the mixture.
4. Arrange the walnuts on the pan in a single layer and bake for 15 minutes, then toss and bake for another 20 minutes, until the nuts are golden and the coating is dry.
5. Let cool completely and serve or store in an airtight container at room temperature for up to 2 weeks.

233

RECIPES

cheesy basil garlic bread

Bread is one of my true loves, and the capacity for its versatility is endless. Have you ever used a cheesy garlic bread as the base of your sandwich creations? That's what we're doing with this recipe, featured on That Sandwich Sampler Plate. The fragrant garlic-and-butter blend with the gooey cheese creates a decadent, savory bite. Try topping this bread with mortadella, banana peppers, and onion to make the ultimate crostini, or play it low-key and serve it by itself!

serves 4 • time: 20 minutes

1 stick (8 tablespoons) salted butter, softened

3 garlic cloves, minced

1 teaspoon onion powder

Freshly ground black pepper to taste

2 tablespoons chopped fresh basil

1 (10-ounce) loaf of French bread, halved lengthwise

8 ounces (2 cups) shredded mozzarella

1. Preheat the oven to 400°F. Line a sheet pan with parchment paper or foil.
2. In a small bowl, stir together the butter, garlic, onion powder, black pepper, and 1½ tablespoons of the basil until smooth.
3. Place the bread on the sheet pan. Evenly spread the butter mixture on each side of the bread. Top each half with 1 cup of the mozzarella.
4. Bake for 10 to 12 minutes, until the cheese has melted and the bread is light golden.
5. Top with the remaining basil, slice into thick pieces, and serve immediately.

warm stuffed dates with blue cheese, speck, and candied ginger

AS SEEN ON THAT CHEESE DATE PLATE

These hot dates are a great pairing for your hot date night. The combination of blue cheese, ginger, and speck adds a dimension to your cheese plate that's bursting with flavor. Dates are one of my favorite ways to add some natural sweetness to a dish. They pair wonderfully with cheese, especially my favorite—a pungent blue, for contrast. Speck is a lightly smoked Italian ham with a savory, salty flavor. Altogether, this dish makes for an unforgettable moment.

makes 12 dates · time: 15 minutes

12 whole Medjool dates

4 ounces blue cheese

4 slices Italian speck

½ ounce (about 1 tablespoon) crystallized ginger, chopped

Fresh thyme leaves, for garnish

1. Preheat the oven to 375°F. Line a sheet pan with parchment paper.
2. Slice the dates in half lengthwise, but not completely through, and open up. Remove the pits and discard.
3. Divide the blue cheese and speck evenly among the dates and place on the lined sheet pan.
4. Bake for 10 to 12 minutes, until the dates are warm and the cheese is soft and bubbling.
5. Top each date with a piece or two of crystallized ginger and a few thyme leaves. Let cool slightly and serve warm.

237

RECIPES

salted caramel and chocolate popcorn clusters

Popcorn and marshmallows, surprisingly, make for a great cheese pairing, especially partnered with sweet chocolate and caramel. Seek out cheeses with notes of vanilla, toasted nuts, and sea salt to pair with this recipe, like a toma (Italian cow's milk farmhouse cheese), blueberry vanilla goat cheese, or a French brie.

makes 16 popcorn balls • time: 15 minutes

2 tablespoons extra-virgin olive oil

10 cups popped popcorn (¼ to ⅔ cup popcorn kernels, depending on the brand)

3 tablespoons salted butter

10 ounces mini marshmallows

½ teaspoon vanilla extract

3 fun-size caramel-and-chocolate bars, such as Twix or Snickers, chopped

⅓ cup yellow and orange chocolate M&Ms

¼ cup dark chocolate chips, melted

Flaky salt, for garnish

1. In a large pot set over medium heat, warm the olive oil. Add 2 popcorn kernels and cover the pot until they pop. Off the heat, add the remaining kernels. Cover the pot and shake it to coat the kernels in oil. Return to the heat and cook, shaking the pot occasionally, until all the kernels have popped. Place the popcorn in a large bowl.

2. In a large skillet over medium-high heat, melt the butter. Add the mini marshmallows and stir with a wooden spoon frequently for about 3 minutes, until melted and creamy. Add the vanilla and stir to combine.

3. Remove the skillet from the heat and pour the mixture over the popcorn. Mix until fully coated.

4. Allow to set for 1 minute, then stir in the chopped candy bars.

5. Line a sheet pan or large plate with parchment paper. Wash and dry your hands, then lightly grease them with olive oil. Separate the popcorn into 3-inch balls and press the M&Ms onto the exterior. Drizzle with the melted chocolate chips and sprinkle with flaky salt.

6. Allow the balls to set for an hour before serving. Do not put them in the refrigerator or they will get soggy.

7. Store in an airtight container for up to 2 days.

fig, sweet onion, and rosemary jam

This recipe adds some dimension to classic fig preserves, making for a wonderfully sweet, savory, and herbaceous pairing for cheeses like Manchego, vintage cheddar, and aged gouda. The addition of sautéed onions and rosemary creates a flavor that can also stand up to salty charcuterie like prosciutto and jamon Iberico. You can make your fig jam from scratch, but fresh figs are a bit hard to find all year round. I decided to elevate a store-bought jam and it turned out delicious!

makes 1 cup • time: 10 minutes

1 tablespoon extra-virgin olive oil

½ cup chopped sweet onion

1 garlic clove, minced

1 tablespoon chopped fresh rosemary leaves, plus more for garnish

Kosher salt and freshly ground black pepper

1 (8½-ounce) jar of fig jam

1 teaspoon fresh lemon juice

1. In a medium saucepan, warm the olive oil over medium heat. Add the onion and garlic and sauté for 5 minutes, stirring occasionally, until translucent and almost golden. Add the rosemary, season to taste with salt and pepper, and sauté for an additional minute.
2. Stir the fig jam and lemon juice into the onion, garlic, and rosemary. Cook, stirring, for 1 to 2 minutes, until thoroughly combined and bubbling.
3. Pour the jam into a heatproof, airtight container and let fully cool in the refrigerator before serving. When ready to serve, garnish with additional rosemary. Store in the refrigerator for up to 2 weeks.

drinks

It's time to elevate your cheese experience with a delicious beverage. While wine and cheese are often said to be the perfect match, there's a whole world of drinks out there that pair wonderfully with cheese. I love to think outside the box here, pairing cheese with different cocktails, beer, and nonalcoholic beverages. Drinks add a new layer of dimension to a pairing. Just as cherry compote pairs wonderfully with nutty, aged cheeses, a Manhattan with Luxardo cherries can transform your bite of aged gouda into a flavorful party.

In this chapter, I included a few personal go-to cocktails (each recipe makes one drink), and asked some of my favorite people in the cheese world to share their ideal cocktail and cheese pairing—like a cocktail potluck!

lavender rosé wine spritzer

PAIR WITH: FETA

I always love a classic wine spritzer with a cheese plate. For this cocktail, lavender simple syrup spruces things up with floral notes. This drink is perfect for springtime gatherings or summer picnics. The rosé and lavender combination is an excellent sweet and herbal contrast to the salty, briny feta. Garnish with rose petals for a beautiful finishing detail!

makes: 1 drink

8 ounces chilled rosé wine

½ tablespoon fresh lemon juice

½ tablespoon lavender simple syrup

¼ cup soda water

Edible rose petals and fresh lavender, for garnish

1. Fill a wineglass with cubed ice. Fill with rosé, followed by the lemon juice and lavender simple syrup. Fill with soda water to the top.
2. Garnish with rose petals and lavender.

MAKE IT A MOCKTAIL: Replace the rosé with seltzer and a splash of cranberry juice.

245

DRINKS

rosemary grapefruit smoky paloma

Palomas are one of my go-to cocktails. If, like me, you find margaritas too sweet, you'll like the tartness of the grapefruit juice used here. The bubbles of the soda water mixed with smoky mezcal and fresh rosemary makes for a fresh yet sultry cocktail.

makes: 1 drink

2 sprigs fresh rosemary

1½ ounces rosemary-infused mezcal
(or tequila blanco for a nonsmoky
option)

1 tablespoon fresh lime juice

3 ounces fresh grapefruit juice

¼ cup soda water

1. In a shaker, muddle the leaves from 1 sprig of rosemary.
2. Add the mezcal, lime juice, and grapefruit juice to the shaker along with cubed ice.
3. Shake well for 30 seconds.
4. Double-strain into a pint glass filled with cubed ice, top with soda water, and garnish with the second rosemary sprig.

MAKE IT A MOCKTAIL: Substitute ½ teaspoon liquid smoke for the mezcal and add another splash of grapefruit juice. Top the rest with soda water.

madame fromage's bijou

"One of my favorite gin cocktail and cheese pairings is a Bijou and a Bijou! A Bijou is a pale green sipper, very herbaceous, that pairs beautifully with young goat cheese—in this case a little cushion of Bijou from Vermont Creamery. It's all about bright herbaceous flavors in the glass and in the cheese."

—Tenaya Darlington, cheese educator and author (@MadameFromage)

makes: 1 drink

1½ ounces gin

¾ ounce green Chartreuse

1 ounce bianco vermouth

2 dashes orange bitters

1. Stir all ingredients in a mixing glass or cocktail shaker with ice and strain into a chilled coupe glass.

247

DRINKS

cheese gal's dirty martini

"This dirty martini recipe has the *perfect* amount of saltiness and a beautiful richness in flavor from the blue cheese; you will be certain that it really is the most delicious martini you've ever had. Obviously, you've got to pair this with a decadent blue cheese."

—*Cortney LaCorte, founder of @CheeseGal*

makes: 1 drink

High-quality blue cheese (some domestic favorites: Bayley Hazen Blue, Bay Blue, Maytag Blue, Rogue River Blue)

3 ounces Belvedere vodka, plus a splash for the cheese

5 Mezzetta Colossal Castelvetrano Style Whole Olives

Dolin vermouth

5 tablespoons juice from the Mezzetta olives, or to taste

1. Place a martini glass in the freezer while you stuff the olives.
2. To make the blue cheese olives, place 2 ounces of the blue cheese into a bowl and add a splash of vodka. Mix together with a fork, and place into a plastic sandwich bag. Cut a slit into the bottom corner and pipe the mixture into the pitted olives.
3. Take the martini glass out of the freezer, rinse the glass with Dolin vermouth, discard the excess, and place back in the freezer.
4. Pour the 3 ounces vodka and olive juice into a cocktail shaker full of ice. (You can adjust the olive juice based on how dirty you want your cocktail.)
5. Shake the cocktail shaker until frosted and pour into the martini glass.
6. Garnish with the blue cheese–stuffed olives.

erika's mom's gin & tonic

"All those fizzy bubbles cut right through the rich cheese, while the gin teases out the botanic flavors in the sheep's milk. My mom always spruces up this classic drink with extra garnishes, which amplify the herbaceous notes."

—*Erika Kubick, Cheese Preacher*
(@CheeseSexDeath)

makes: 1 drink

2 ounces gin

1 lemon slice

4 to 6 juniper berries

4 ounces Fever-Tree tonic water

1 sprig of thyme, for garnish

1. Fill a highball glass with ice.
2. Pour in the gin, then add the lemon and juniper berries.
3. Top with the tonic water and give it a few gentle stirs.
4. Slap the thyme sprig between your palms to release the aroma before garnishing the drink.

249

DRINKS

kalimotxo 2.0

"I love how the caramel and dark cherry notes in this Coca-Cola-based highball really punch up Sunny Ridge's latent stone fruit flavors while providing a bubbly textural contrast to its paste. Feel free to pair Kalimotxos with other bright, washed-rind goat cheeses, Manchego, or your favorite Basque cheese. Enjoy with olives on a lazy summer afternoon by the lake. *Topa!*"

—*Alisha Norris Jones, cheesemonger at
Immortal Milk (@_immortalmilk)*

makes: 1 drink

1½ ounces red wine, preferably
Lambrusco

½ ounce Punt e Mes (or any sweet
Italian vermouth)

¼ ounce Fernet-Branca

1 tablespoon lime juice

2 dashes Angostura bitters

2 tablespoons soda water

3 tablespoons Coca-Cola, preferably
bottled Mexican Coca-Cola

2 orange slices, to garnish

1. Combine the red wine, Punt e Mes, Fernet-Branca, lime juice, and bitters in a cocktail shaker and add ice.
2. Shake until chilled.
3. Strain into an ice-filled highball glass (or a mason jar), then top with the soda water and Coca-Cola.
4. Garnish with 2 orange slices.

lady spritz

"Dry vermouth is complex and floral on the nose, which pairs gloriously with the salty savoriness of this sheep milk cheese."

— *Sarah Simms, co-founder of Lady and Larder*
(@ladyandlarder)

makes: 1 drink

2 ounces dry vermouth (like
    Lo-Fi Aperitifs)

½ cup Topo Chico sparkling
    mineral water

Flowering coriander blossom or
    orange peel, for garnish

1. Fill a rocks glass with ice.
2. Add the dry vermouth, then top with sparkling water. Gently stir to combine.
3. Garnish with a coriander blossom or orange peel.

251

DRINKS

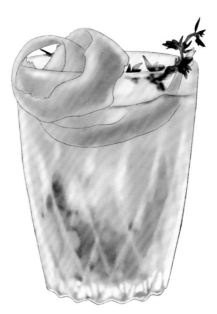

jim's signature manhattan

"I prefer my Manhattan slightly less sweet, and always use what I consider to be one of the best vermouths, Antica Formula, which dates back to the 1700s. It matches up perfectly with my choice of either Michter's single-barrel straight rye whiskey or Woodford Reserve bourbon. The Luxardo cherries are soaked in a rich syrup that makes a perfect subtle sweetener. I love to pair this with a nutty and rich aged gouda."

—Jim Mullen (my dad)

makes: 1 drink

4 ounces high-quality rye or single-batch bourbon

1 ounce Antica Formula sweet vermouth

2 to 3 dashes Angostura orange bitters

Luxardo cherries or orange peel, for garnish

1. Fill a coupe or martini glass with ice and water and chill in the freezer for 10 minutes.
2. Stir the bourbon, vermouth, and bitters in a mixing glass with ice, or mix in a shaker with ice.
3. Empty the ice and strain into the chilled glass and garnish with cherries. As an alternative to the cherries, rub the rim of the glass with a small piece of orange peel and add to the drink.

ellen's basil, mint, and cucumber gimlet

"I make this cocktail with fresh herbs and cucumbers from my garden in the summer, and it's the most refreshing drink. The combination of the basil and mint brings out the herbaceous notes in the gin, making for a wonderful pairing with soft cheeses like fresh mozzarella."

—*Ellen Mullen (my mom)*

makes: 1 drink

2-inch piece of peeled cucumber, quartered

5 mint leaves, plus 1 sprig, for garnish

5 basil leaves

1 tablespoon simple syrup

1½ tablespoons lime juice

2½ ounces gin

1. In a cocktail shaker, muddle the cucumber with the mint leaves, basil, and simple syrup.
2. Fill the shaker with ice, then pour in the lime juice and gin.
3. Shake for about 30 seconds, until the cocktail is chilled.
4. Strain into a coupe glass and garnish with a sprig of mint

MAKE IT A MOCKTAIL: Replace the gin and simple syrup with ½ tablespoon of juniper simple syrup. Once shaken, pour into a glass and fill with soda water.

253

DRINKS

guide to wine and cheese pairings

Many would assume that wine and cheese are the perfect match, but that's not always the case! For example, a big, bold red will completely drown out the nuances of a light and delicate goat cheese, and a sharp, pungent blue will overshadow the flavor of a dry, crisp white. Here are some of my wine and cheese pairing tips to help avoid these clashes.

Pair Similar Intensities: A delicate fresh goat cheese will go well with a crisp sauvignon blanc. The light-bodied wine won't overpower the notes of the cheese. If you want to go with a red, try pairing a Stilton with a dessert wine, like port.

Think About Tasting Notes: A pinot noir may have notes of piercing tart red fruits. Think about what cheese you would pair with those fruity aromas. Comté goes wonderfully with a sour cherry jam, so Comté would be a great pairing for pinot noir.

Bubbles and Brie: A prosecco or Champagne goes great with a fatty, creamy cheese like camembert or brie. The bubbles act as a palate cleanser. Sparkling wine is also great with dry, salty cheeses like parmesan, pecorino, and Grana Padano.

Big Bolds with Aged Cheese: A sharp, fruity, umami cheese like smoked gouda, Ossau-Iraty, or vintage cheddar can stand up to a medium- or full-bodied red wine like Bordeaux, merlot, or cabernet sauvignon. The flavors can stand on their own without overpowering each other.

Salty and Funky: A salty cheese like feta or halloumi would pair nicely with a funky orange wine (aka skin-contact white wine). The slightly sweet quince undertone of orange wine makes for a great match with salty Eastern Mediterranean and Middle Eastern cheeses.

Pairings are personal, so do some taste testing—as I always say, if you like it, the pairing works!

257

DRINKS

cheesy party games

What's a party without some games! Here are a few ideas to get the vibes going.

that cheese deck

I created this game as a nod to the drinking game Kings (oh, college), but instead of drinking, we eat the cheese plate. Also, the rules are completely different. Take a deck of playing cards and arrange them around the cheese plate, face down. Each person takes a turn, picking a card. Each card has an activity. See next page for the key!

2 — Make a curated bite from the cheese plate for someone of your choice.

3 — Make a curated bite from the cheese plate for yourself.

4 — Restock the crackers on the cheese plate.

5 — Pair a cheese with a drink of choice.

6 — Take an artsy photo of the cheese plate (and tag @ThatCheesePlate on Instagram if you want).

7 — Make a mystery bite with your eyes closed.

8 — Pick a date (you eat any bite they eat).

9 — Phone a friend (call someone at random and ask their favorite cheese).

10 — Round of Categories (cheese puns, cheese of France, types of charcuterie, etc.).

J — Refill the drinks.

Q — Make up a poem on the spot about the cheese plate.

K — Share one thing you're grateful for.

A — Compliment the host.

BYO pairing party

This one is easy: bring your own pairing! Have each guest bring their favorite cheese and cheese accompaniment. For example, I'd bring a nicely aged pecorino with prosciutto. Arrange all the pairings on a board and take turns trying each one.

cheesy dress party

Encourage your guests to dress up as their favorite cheese! This can be as simple or as creative as you want. Hold a best-dressed awards at the end of the night (with cheese prizes, naturally).

all together now

The table is set, the cheese is plated, and you're ready to host! Whether you're hanging at home by yourself with your favorite wedge of cheese, or with a group of loved ones celebrating a big milestone, relish in the present. By coming together in a positive and creative way, these moments of connection are times to never take for granted. Cheese is the gateway to deeper conversations, laughter, reflection, and love. It's a common ground for all walks of life. So, turn on your favorite playlist, pour yourself a tasty drink, and dive into That Cheese Plate. It's time to party!

ACKNOWLEDGMENTS

I am so grateful for everyone who has supported That Cheese Plate over the years. Thank you for coming to my cheese classes, making plates from my first cookbook, wearing my cheese merch, and spreading positivity through cheese every day. I would not be able to have this career without your love and encouragement. Every cheese plate you tag me in makes me feel so inspired!

This book goes out to all of my dear friends, you know who you are! Thank you for being my soul family, taking all my leftover cheese, and letting me text you every plate photo for approval. We've had the craziest cheese parties, and you are the best support system a gal could have.

To That Cheese Team and everyone who helped with the creation of this book: Clio Seraphim, Eve Attermann, Whitney Frick, Jenna Praeger, Sara Gilanchi, Alex Najarian, Noel McGrath, Victoria Nadler from Amber Sol Collective, Rebecca Frisker, Rachel Schwartz, and everyone behind the scenes at WME, The Dial Press, and Random House—thanks for all of your constant support and hustle with this book and beyond.

Jim, Ellen, Shayne, Nikki, and all of my family and family-friends, I love you and thank you for continuously cheering on my crazy ventures. Our gatherings at holiday celebrations, pool parties, beach barbecues, and family vacations inspired many of the plates in this book.

This book is in honor of Anne Saxelby, the true queen of cheese. Anne pioneered the artisanal local cheese movement in the United States, highlighting makers and farmers from across the country at her cheese shop, Saxelby's Cheese in Manhattan. Please consider donating to the Anne Saxelby Legacy Fund, which builds programs for youth to apprentice in sustainable systems and agriculture, domestically and abroad, at https://www.annesaxelbylegacyfund.org.

INDEX

265

INDEX

271

MARISSA MULLEN is a bestselling author, entrepreneur, content creator, and food stylist. She is the founder of That Cheese Plate, a global community for cheese plate inspiration and creative recipes. With her beautiful, inventive, and accessible approach to food styling, she pioneered the cheese plate and charcuterie trend in popular culture today. Her innovative Cheese By Numbers method has revolutionized how cheese and charcuterie boards are crafted, and her work consistently inspires authenticity, intentional gatherings, and finding joy in the present moment.

Mullen has appeared on *The Today Show, Good Morning America, The Rachael Ray Show, Live with Kelly and Ryan, Business Insider,* and *Food and Wine,* among many other outlets. Her debut cookbook, *That Cheese Plate Will Change Your Life,* underscores how creating cheese plates can be a grounding, meditative activity. This book has inspired many, was awarded Amazon's Editor's Pick for 2020, and was listed on *The Wall Street Journal*'s bestseller list.

Marissa is dedicated to bringing people together through creativity, self-expression, and entertaining.

thatcheeseplate.com
marissamullen.com
Instagram: @thatcheeseplate
@cheesebynumbers
@thatcheeseclass
@marissamullen
TikTok: @thatcheeseplate